The Seven Voices of God

The Seven Voices of God

Dr. William H. Goddard

Copyright © 2008 by Dr. William H. Goddard.

ISBN: Softcover   978-1-4363-7594-8

All rights reserved. No part of this book may be reproduced or transmitted in any form or by any means, electronic or mechanical, including photocopying, recording, or by any information storage and retrieval system, without permission in writing from the copyright owner.

This book was printed in the United States of America.

To order additional copies of this book, contact:
Xlibris Corporation
1-888-795-4274
www.Xlibris.com
Orders@Xlibris.com

Contents

FORWARD	9
AN OLD STORY	11
MY STORY	13
PRELUDE TO A NEW LIFE	15
THE FIRST VOICE OF GOD: THE VOICE OF COMFORT	20
A NEW ASSIGNMENT	30
THE SECOND VOICE OF GOD: THE CALL	31
GRADUATION AND COMMENCEMENT	41
THE SUMMER VACATION WE NEEDED	43
THE THIRD VOICE OF GOD: CHALLENGE	46
A CHANGE IN MY THINKING	49
WE GO WEST TO CALIFORNIA	52
TWO DANCING DAUGHTERS	55
THE FOURTH VOICE OF GOD: COMMAND	57
BIG CHANGES WERE ABOUT TO HAPPEN	61
THE FIFTH VOICE OF GOD: COMMITMENT	64
A BIG DECISION WAS MADE – NOW THE CONSEQUENCES	66
THE SIXTH VOICE OF GOD: COVERING	70
WORKING TOWARD MY DOCTOR'S DEGREE	75
A CHANGE IN MINISTRY	79
THE SEVENTH VOICE OF GOD: CONTEMPLATION	81
LOOKING FOR THE MEANING	84
EPILOGUE	93
POSTSCRIPT	93
REFERENCES	95

DEDICATION

In gratitude and thanksgiving to my Heavenly Father I dedicate this book to

My wife, Beverly, the bride of my youth and the mother of my children who taught me how to be a husband.

My two daughters, Sheryl and Shauna who taught me how to be a father.

My five grandchildren, Calico, Dash, Sonora, Christopher and Sophia who continue to teach me that there is so much more to learn

The congregations in Colorado and Connecticut who were helpful in the process of teaching me how to be a pastor.

The congregations in California and Illinois who allowed me to share with them what I had learned.

FORWARD

EVERY THING BEGINS with the Word of God. God speaks everything into existence. With God Word and deed go together. Whatever God says, He does. When God said: "Let there be light", there was light.

God's Word is powerful. His Word can lift up or bring down. His Word is never weak or wavering. His Word is truthful and trustworthy. When God speaks, something happens.

I have heard God speak to me seven times.

This is a personal story of my life and ministry with particular focus on my reaction to the seven times I know that God spoke to me.

When I say "spoke", I mean that literally. He spoke words that I could hear in my ear and comprehend with my mind. The number seven is not to be understood as symbolic of anything in any way. I do not list the number seven because it is the "perfect number", or because it is used so often in the Bible.

The number seven just happens to be the number of times that I have heard the voice of God to challenge, change, or encourage me. In only one instance was His voice in answer to prayer. The other six times were not only unexpected and somewhat surprising, they shook my very being.

What I am relating in the pages which follow is my personal account of events that shaped my life and ministry. Since it is personal, I am hesitant to involve others in this account. To be both fair and honest, however, I must name dates and places in order for you to understand why and how I reacted to hearing . . . . yes, hearing with my physical ears, the articulate and clear voice of God.

I want it understood at the beginning that I am not writing this to claim any exclusivity in my relationship with God. I am no prophet or the son of a prophet. I do not know why these occurrences happened, only that they did.

In reflecting on these events, I am reminded of a reputed conversation between Joan of Arc and the Dauphine who questioned Joan's statement that "God speaks to me" with the retort:

"Why should God speak to you and not to me, I am the Dauphine." Joan's reply was: "He does speak to you, your majesty, but you hear the angelus ring and cross yourself, and go on with your life. You do not listen."

I would add that God speaks when we are not listening or expecting Him to speak. I know that the Bible is the written Word of God given to us over the bridge of time. But God is not limited to the printed page. He speaks to whom He will, where He chooses.

The time span over which I have heard God speak to me is sixty-four years. I must add that while I am not expecting to hear from Him again, I did not expect to hear His voice in the first place. I never know what will prompt His direct intervention in my life. Perhaps you have experienced that very thing in your life also.

This is my account as I remember these seven times I have heard this direct voice of God. Each one had an impact on me in ways I could never have expected. You will learn, also, that I have not always been obedient to His voice. Now, on with the story.

AN OLD STORY

THERE IS A remarkable story in the Old Testament about a man named Samuel. He is known as the first person to be a prophet, a judge, and a priest. In fact, Samuel is called the first prophet and the last judge of Israel. His was a fruitful life with a strange beginning. You can read about his early life in the first three chapters of I Samuel in the Bible.

Samuel was the answer to a desperate woman's prayer. The woman's name was Hannah. She was married to Elkanah. For many years Hanna desired to become a mother, but she was barren. Year after year she and her husband journeyed from their home in Ramathaim to Shiloah. That was where the Ark of the Covenant was placed in a tabernacle. Eli was the priest of Shiloah. It was to Shiloah that Hannah and Elkanah would go to pray and to bring an offering to the Lord.

On one such journey, after the offering was made and hours of prayer, Hannah was in fervent prayer asking God for a son. She promised to return her son to God's service if God would grant her the desire of her heart.

Eli, the priest, could not hear Hannah's words but he knew that she was in ardent prayer. Eli spoke these words to her as she and her husband were leaving:

"Go in peace, and may the God of Israel grant you what you have asked of Him."

In due time God did answer Hannah's prayer. She gave birth to a son whom she named Samuel, a name which means 'called of God'. Hannah named her son Samuel because, she said, "I asked the Lord for him."

Hannah was true to her vow and after the boy was old enough to walk, she returned to Shiloah and presented Samuel as a gift to God to be raised by Eli the priest. She gave back to God the gift that God had given to her.

For her faithfulness God granted to her in the following years three sons and two daughters.

Each year Hannah brought a new garment to Samuel who grew up beside Eli in the tabernacle at Shiloah.

One night, a few years after Samuel's arrival at Shiloah, while he was sleeping, God awakened Samuel and called to him by name.

Not knowing who had called him, Samuel went to Eli's bed and said:

"Here I am."

Eli, now advanced in years with poor eyesight and failing hearing, told Samuel to go back to bed, that he had not called Samuel.

This same sequence was repeated twice with the same response from Eli. Then, upon reflection, Eli realized that the voice Samuel heard was the Lord's voice.

Eli then said: "Go and lie down, and if He calls you, say 'Speak, Lord, for your servant is listening.'"

The Bible tells us that God not only spoke to Samuel that night, but

> "The Lord was with Samuel as he grew up, and He let none of his words fall to the ground. And all Israel from Dan to Beersheba recognized that Samuel was attested as a prophet of the Lord and the Lord revealed Himself to Samuel through the word."
> (I Samuel 3: 19-21)

MY STORY

Let's Start At The Very Beginning

I WAS BORN in Waco, Texas, the fourth of five children, during the Depression in 1933. At this time there were only four of us. My younger brother, Jim, would arrive five years later.

My first memory of life in the church my family attended was as a five year old kindergartner. My sister had taken me to a Baptist church where she and her teenage friends were part of a large youth group. I was placed in a Sunday School room where children from Kindergarden to Second grade were taught. I had been to this church before and felt very much at home. But, I was somewhat of a showoff and said something that angered two large first graders. One of them told me, under his breath, that as soon as this class was over they were "going to get me."

As class was dismissed I ran out the door and into the hallway being followed quickly by these two angry first graders. I wondered as I ran why they were so upset, but reasons did not matter now and this was not the time to pause and reflect. I ran down one hallway, then another. The boys were still in pursuit.

I rounded a corner and saw a stairway leading up. I went up. At the top of the stairs I found my self standing in a shallow, concrete pit. On the other side of the pit were stairs leading down. As I started to go down those stairs I beheld one of the first graders, standing at the bottom. Turning to go back the way I had come, I saw the other first grader standing at the bottom. Trapped.

As I turned to my right there was a blank wall with a cross hanging on it and to the left were heavy, red velvet drapes. My only hope was through those drapes. I flung them back from the middle and immediately heard an audible gasp from a crowd of people in the sanctuary.

Unknowingly, I had run into the baptistry during the morning worship hour. Now, standing in that shallow pit, looking over a glass panel I saw only two familiar faces. The first one was that of my 16 year old sister, Edith, who was seated with her girl friends. The look on her face was not comforting to me. Her eyes were wide, her mouth was open and her hands flew upward in shock as she saw the five year old she had brought to church interrupting the service and embarrassing her before her friends. No help there.

The second face I recognized was that of the pastor who had turned from the pulpit to stare into the eyes of a frightened five-year old who had disrupted the service. Being afraid of the fate which awaited me if the two first graders got their hands on me, I yelled out to the pastor: "BROTHER BOSWELL, ... BROTHER BOSWELL, . . . SAVE ME, SAVE ME!"

At this time my two adversaries disappeared. In their place was a very large man in a white suit, with red hair and a red face who reached into the baptistry and with rough, strong hands lifted me up to the level of his face, looked me in the eyes and said those words which chilled my soul: "BOY . . . . I KNOOOOW YOUUUR PARRENTS."

Surprisingly enough that first episode in church did not deter my continued attendance. From the age of four I was raised in the church.

Like Samuel, I am a product of the church. Unlike Samuel, I did not have a mentor or spiritual guide over the next eight years of my life. When I was six years old my family, now with my year old brother, moved from Texas to Alabama, then to Georgia.

It was in Alabama that God first spoke to me in a Voice I actually heard.

PRELUDE TO A NEW LIFE

ONE SUNDAY, WHEN I was 12 years old, I was seated at the end of a pew in the Bealwood Baptist Church in Columbus, Georgia. The morning worship service had not begun and I was talking with a friend. I felt a hand on my shoulder. Looking up I saw the pastor who had stopped on his way to the pulpit.

He said, "Isn't it time for you to be baptized?" This was the first person to ask about my spiritual state. I had no other answer than "Yes."

I attended a month of Sunday classes with about 14 other youngsters my age preparing for baptism and membership in the church. Most of the class members were girls, with about six boys. When the day came for our baptism we took a trip to a large downtown Baptist church with a great baptistry – much larger than the one I had first stood in as a five-year old in Texas.

The girls were baptized first while the boys waited in another room. When it was time for us to be baptized we all entered the room where before us stretched a huge auditorium with an enormous balcony in the back, and a voluminous choir loft below us. The baptistry was large enough for us all to stand around as the pastor baptized each one.

When it was my turn, the pastor addressed me: "Billy, do you receive Jesus Christ as your Savior and Lord? Will you be obedient to Him for the rest of your life?"

"Yes", I replied. "Then", he said, "I baptize you in the name of the Father, and the Son and the Holy Ghost." Whereupon I was plunged into the water.

I could not find the proper words to describe what happened to me then, at that moment in time. I knew .... I felt ... I believe ... I know ... at that moment something tremendous happened in my life. Now, I can say that, like Samuel, my name was known to God.

"What was that?", I said as I was lifted from the water by the pastor.

Those standing around the pool asked "What are you talking about?"

"Didn't you feel that?", I asked.

"Yeah", one of them said, "We are all wet, we feel that."

"No, No." I replied Didn't something just happen?" "Yes", another boy replied, "You're just as wet as the rest of us. Come on, we are going swimming."

But I knew that what had just happened to me was something unique. When I arose from those waters of baptism God's Holy Spirit filled me with His resurrection power. I became a new creature in Christ. The old had passed away. The new had come.

I did not realize any of this at that time, however. I continued my childish ways with little time for personal prayer.

My Bible study was done in compliance with what was expected in the Sunday School Classes. I would study to prepare for Bible quizzes in class and for Bible Drills in Vacation Bible School. I could name the books of the Bible, and Jesus' disciples and recount some of His miracles, but the significance of my new personhood was neither realized or fully appreciated by me.

At the time of my birth in Waco, Texas my father was in a Veterans' Hospital. He was an Army veteran of World War I. While fighting with his Army unit against the Germans, his unit suffered a mustard gas attack. This had long range consequences which necessitated frequent stays in the hospital for treatment.

Another factor in his poor health was a bullet which had entered his side, but was too close to the spinal cord for surgery in those early years. The doctors watched as the bullet made its way through his soft tissue, waiting to perform an operation to remove the bullet once it was safer to do so.

My father was to die at the age of 57 with that bullet still in him after 34 years.

It was my sister, Edith, who told me of our family history before my birth. As I remember her account of what happened to them she told me:

> When the Great Depression hit our country in the late 1920's and early 1930's my father had a partner in the Dry Cleaning Business. They had a large establishment in Alabama with a fleet of trucks to pick up and deliver clothes to be cleaned. Mother, Father, Roy, the first born son, Edith, the only girl in the family, and Jack, the second son, lived in their own home with all the comforts attendant to a prosperous businessman, complete with an automobile. Then came the Stock Market Crash of 1929. Debts where called in by the bank. My father's partner left town. My father sold the business, lost the trucks, house and car. We were broke and father's health was made all the worse. The family had to be separated for several months. My father went in the hospital, Roy, Edith and Jack each went to live with mother's sisters. These three siblings were not able to see each other for weeks at a time. Upon my father's release from the hospital, father decided to move his family to Texas where he had relatives who offered our family housing.

Dad went back into the dry cleaning business; not as an owner but as the manager of a large firm in Waco, Texas. It was there I was born November, 1933.

During the first three years of my life, according to my sister, we moved thee times.

From those early years of my childhood I brought two physical scars into adulthood.

The first scar was the result of an accident when I was 11 months old. My sister had found a round Lipton Tea can with a top which could be taken off and put back on. She had filled the can with buttons and placed the top back on. I used this as my first toy.

The house we lived in had a large porch with several steps leading up from the walkway. I was just learning to walk and would roll the can across the porch, then walk to get it.

One day I pushed the can too far. It rolled down the steps, the top came off, and it rested on the walkway with the sharp edges up. In my haste to get the can I tootled to the steps, and before Edith could stop me, tumbled down the steps and landed with my face on the sharp edge of the can.

My lip was cut through to the gum, with only one bit of skin holding my lip to my face. The doctor told the family that if he stitched my lip in place that it would become distorted as I grew. He put my lip back in place and secured in by adhesive tape. It worked.

My lip was saved, but the scar is there to this day.

My second physical scar came on the first day of my entrance into second grade.

It was time for recess. The teacher dismissed the girls to the playground and the boys were to go the ball field. Before she let us leave the room she called me back to give me a football with these instructions:

"Billy, you are in charge of the boys football game. You are to choose up sides and play touch football. Remember, Billy, no tackling."

We ran to the ball field and chose sides. Before my side kicked the ball to the other team I said:

"What are we? We are not sissies. Let's play tackle." No one spoke. We kicked the football to the other team. The largest boy on that team caught the ball and started running toward us.

"Tackle him, tackle him, I shouted." "You tackle him". shouted one of my team mates. You are the one who wanted to play tackle football. The teacher said no tackling."

What was I to do? As this large boy ran past me I reached out and grabbed his foot. As we fell to the ground his heel clipped one of my lower front teeth. The front part of that tooth came off. There was instant pain.

From that day to this that tooth has been sensitive. Over the years I have had several dentists offer to smooth the tooth off and fill the gap there. Every time I refused.

Each time I run my tongue over that rough spot I remind myself of the penalty of disobedience.

My mouth has caused me some trouble over the years. I have the scars to prove it.

Don't forget a scarred lip and a chipped tooth.

In 1938 my younger brother, James Eugene, was born. My oldest brother, Roy joined the Navy. My brother Jack, two years younger than Roy, persuaded our father to let him drop out of school at the age of 17 to join the Navy also. Money was short and jobs were scarce. Dad signed the papers for Jack to join his brother in the Navy.

As the decade of the 1940's began we moved back to Alabama. Jim and I are the only siblings born in Texas.

As World War II raged in both Europe and the Pacific, mother joined the "Navy Mothers Club" and put a flag with two blue stars in our front window. Everything in our family life revolved around the War. Jim and I collected newspapers and tin cans for recycling.

The two of us would, however, go the the Saturday movie matinee with our 16 cent weekly allowance. We would then act out over the next week the action scenes from the movie we had just seen.

I can remember being the Lone Ranger, the Green Hornet and Tarzan. Jim, because he was five years younger, was relegated to be my side kick. He was Tonto to my Lone Ranger and Kayto to my Green Hornet. He refused, however, to be the Jane to my Tarzan.

At the height of the War my father returned us to Texas where he had been called as part of the War Effort to manage the water treatment plant of Dow Chemical Company next to an Army Base near Houston, Texas.

As a ten year-old I sold the local newspaper, "The Houston Chronicle", to earn a few pennies to spend in riotous living: which meant bubble gum when it could be found and an occasional candy bar.

As the War ended we moved back to Alabama. My sister married a young Army Airman and moved out of the house. Both of my older brothers, Roy and Jack, returned from the Navy with scars of their own. Roy was on the aircraft carrier "Hornet" which transported Jimmy Dolittle and his squadron to bomb Tokyo. He was on board when the "Hornet" was sunk by Japanese bombers. Jack was in the boiler room of the "USS Long Island" when the boiler exploded

Added to those physical scars were emotional ones. Both of them had married, then divorced.

My father changed jobs several more times during the following years.

THE FIRST VOICE OF GOD: THE VOICE OF COMFORT

MY FIRST CONSCIOUS memory of hearing God speak to me occurred as my father and I were driving one summer night in his car in Alabama.

I was a 14 year-old teenager who was conflicted and confused about the meaning of life and proper relationships.

I "looked like a love-sick puppy" according to my father. I had my head on the edge of the passenger door, the wind blowing my hair as I stared at the moon on this clear summer night.

I guess I was "a love-sick puppy", I admitted to my father. "You see", I said, "I think I am in love." "With whom?" I named the girl.

He just laughed. This did not feel right to me. I had questions which needed answers. I felt my father did not take me seriously. I wanted to know the purpose of life and where we had come from, and what we were doing here. I really felt alone and little regarded.

We had moved so often that I had no friends, no one with whom to talk. I was feeling unconnected and unappreciated. I had gained so much weight over the last year that I had been taken to a doctor to see if I had some thyroid problem.

I did not know who I was anymore.

It was in that dark and dismal moment that God spoke to me these words:

"IT DOES NOT MATTER HOW YOU GOT HERE. IT IS TO WHOM YOU BELONG NOW."

The most amazing thing happened. As I heard those words, clearly spoken to my ears, I felt my body being lifted out of the car seat! I was stunned . . . . I was speechless . . . I can remember being both confused and comforted.

Who said that? It was not the wind blowing through my hair. It was a clear voice spoken in my ear as I leaned on the passenger side of the front seat of an automobile being driven by my father on a summer night in Alabama. I was startled, surprised, and amazed.

Why had not my father heard the voice? It was certainly loud enough. But he did not hear a thing. Those words were for my ears only.

Suddenly, everything seemed right. I remembered that same feeling when I was baptized two years earlier. I had no way then to explain my feeling, and no one with whom to share them.

Now I knew that these words, spoken to me as we drove that one particular night, were given to assure me that I was accepted by my Heavenly Father. He knew my name and loved me even when I did not realize it.

As a 14 year-old teenage boy with all the conflicts and confusion which were both present and yet to come, I was given a peace which has never left me. God loves me. Jesus is with me. His Holy Spirit resides within me.

What an experience to hear God's Voice and word of assurance that I mattered to Him.

My baptism had been, actually, an adoption ceremony. I was God's adopted child. What I understand now is that I had become a Prince because I am a child of the King.

Some changes came into my life with this revelation. I now listened more closely to the pastor's sermons. I prayed with an expectation of being heard on high. I was given the power to resist the temptations that come to every young person – including alcohol and sex. My friends over the coming years expressed a trust in me.

My brother, Jack, returned from the Navy and started going to church. He became a Boy Scout leader and taught me to fish, tie knots, cook a meal over a campfire and, most importantly, he taught me to drive a truck.

He worked at the same dry cleaning plant that my father managed. Jack drove a delivery truck. I worked with him after school. I was driving over the back county roads of Alabama at the age of 14. While I was in school, Jack shared with me his disappointment in failing to finish high school. He encouraged me to take courses that would prepare me for a better life than driving a delivery truck. At his insistence, I learned to type, and took courses in bookkeeping and shorthand.

At age 16, when I got my license, I was driving a school bus every day for two years until my graduation from high school. Can you imagine the trust necessary for a school principal to allow a 16 year old to drive a school bus with over 25 students on board? I wondered if any of the parents knew of my age.

During these high school years I was surrounded by teachers who were committed Christians who became leaders to help shape and mold my growing faith. God really is good, all the time.

My high school baseball coach believed that I was good enough to try out for professional baseball. The St. Louis Cardinals had a farm team in nearby Columbus, Georgia where they were to hold spring tryouts. My coach took me there for a tryout. I lasted two days with the assessment: "Strong arm, good bat, too slow." It was a great experience to test myself against other players. To the best of my knowledge, no one was signed by the Cardinals at that tryout.

As the decade of the 1950's began, events in distant parts of the world brought changes even to rural Alabama. I graduated high school in May, 1952 and very soon thereafter got the notice that I was going to be drafted into the Army. The conflict in Korea was demanding more men be sent to the fighting lines.

Knowing that without a college deferment, and with no plans for college, I decided to join the United States Air Force. I left home on February 7th, 1953, my first time away from both my parents. The new recruits were flown to San Antiono for two months of basic training. Since the Korean war was still going on, I was transfered to Lowry Air Force Base near Denver, Colorado to begin training to be a gunner on a B-29 aircraft.

I arrived at Lowry Air Force Base, near Denver, Colorado, from San Antonio, Texas on a Friday in April. It was snowing. It had been snowing for several days. It was cold. I was a newly promoted Airman 3rd Class with no privileges attendant to that rank.

I was assigned to a "transit" barracks – which means a temporary place to stay – until the proper housing connected to the school I was to attend was ready for the new arrivals. In that barracks there was no one in charge to make bed assignment or to keep the furnace going. Of the 84 men housed there, no one wanted to keep the coal – fired furnace going. Several of us took turns at the task but it was still cold.

Each of us who had arrived from a warmer climate had our khaki uniforms on and immediately emptied our duffle bags to find warmer clothes to wear. That first night I could not keep warm, even after piling most of my clothes on top of the blanket the whole night.

The next day was Saturday. I went to the Base Exchange to buy some essentials and to inquire about the location of a Baptist Church. I learned that a city bus from Denver made a stop at the Main Gate every half-hour except on Sundays when the schedule was uncertain. I was determined to find a place of worship where I could not only join an assembly of believers, but to enter into a fellowship where the Word of God was expounded and hymns of faith sung.

Early Sunday morning I jumped out of bed into the chilly air and on to the cold floor of the barracks. I probably set a personal record for the time it took getting dressed. The hot water in the bathroom was only warm. I shaved with trembling hands and was surprised to find fewer cuts on my face than I had expected. It was eight o'clock in the morning and I was the only one up.

I walked to the Main Gate through snow over my shoe-tops. Did I mention that it was cold?

After stomping my feet for ten minutes while waiting for the bus, a bus finally arrived. It was 9 o clock when I boarded the bus. No one got off the bus and there was no one else waiting with me.

I boarded an empty bus and immediately found a seat in the middle of the bus under which there was the heater. At last I was getting warm. The driver waited another 5 minutes before leaving the Main Gate with me as the only passenger.

As we drove down Colfax Avenue I looked at the snow covered landscape feeling so out of place while watching neighborhoods and businesses flash by my window. My plan was to go to downtown Denver, find a phone booth, look in the Yellow

Pages for a nearby Baptist Church to attend. The bus made no stops as there was no one standing at the bus stops as we made our way into town.

Suddenly, I was startled to hear footsteps in the aisle behind me and was taken by surprise when a young man sat down beside me. Where had he come from? No one else was on the bus when we left the Main Gate and no stops were made along the way.

His first words to me were "Are you going to church today?"

"Yes I am", I replied.

"Go to church with me," he said.

"Oh no", said I. "I am going to go to a Baptist Church."

"I go to Baptist Church", he stated. "Sure, Okay" was my answer.

Without any more conversation he reached up and pulled the cord to alert the driver to stop at the next bus stop. We disembarked on the corner of Colfax and Fairfax.

I saw no church building. No words were exchanged as we walked. My mind was filled with questions I could not find words to ask. Who was this stranger? When did he get on the bus? What was his name?

The stranger pointed up a hill to the right and we started walking. At least the sidewalk had been cleared of snow for the two blocks we walked. Then, on our right we saw a beautiful little brick church building. We were approaching the back of the building. I could not see a sign indicating the name of the church or the denominational affiliation.

Standing in a partially open doorway stood a short man with wavy black hair and a dazzling smile. His hand was stretched out to us as we came up the walk. He ushered us into the building, explaining that because it was so cold he kept the door partially closed to preserve the heat inside.

The man introduced himself to us as Levi Floyd. It turned out that Mr. Floyd was the teacher of the "College-Career" class which was the class into which we entered. I found out that we were in the City Park Baptist Church and that Dr. Buford Fordham was the pastor.

I was thrilled to be with fellow Christians. Even more thrilled to find that this class had both boys and girls in it. This was the first time in any church I had attended that boys and girls were together to be taught. In all the other Baptist churches I had attended the boys and girls were in separate classes. I liked this class right away, and Mr Floyd was a good teacher.

It turned out that not only was I the only one in uniform, I was the only member of the military in the class. I had yet to learn that one could dress in civilian clothes while off duty.

After the class session was over it was time to go into Worship. Mr Floyd said that since it was cold outside, and there was some snow on the sidewalk to the corner, we should go through the back hallways, through the kitchen, and then into the sanctuary.

I was getting acquainted with some of the class members as we walked down the hallway. I turned to say something to the young man who had brought me to this church and into this class as he was going out the door into which we had come.

I had no name by which to call him, and he was out the door before I could react. I asked several people there if they knew his name.

"No" everyone said. They all said they had never seen him before!

I never saw him again.

Who was this young man who appeared from nowhere, rode the bus, walked me to church and did not even reveal his identity? I have often wondered over the years what would have happened to me that day if I had stayed on the bus alone. I do know that everything would be different in my life.

I have no doubt that young man on the bus was an angel from God, sent to get me off the bus and to the church that would change my life. And change it did.

It was at the City Park Baptist Church of Denver, Colorado in 1953 that I met a beautiful young girl, Beverly Sue Vincent, who consented to be my wife 55 years ago. She has been a constant and consistent encourager to me. She has supported my call to ministry, taught first grade for four years while I attended seminary, and been through countless meetings, cooked copious amounts of casserole dishes, attended numerous Sunday morning classes and worship services, Wednesday night gatherings while raising our two daughters.

There is more to tell about our life together, but, it all began at the City Park Baptist Church in Denver, Colorado on a Sunday morning in April when I was guided by an angel.

It was also at the City Park Baptist Church that the man who met me at the door on that first Sunday, Levi Floyd, I discovered later was in charge of Civilian Personnel at Lowry Air Force Base. Mr Floyd was instrumental in our lives in later years when he helped in ways that only he could have done.

The fellowship of that church which warmed my heart that day continued to be a positive factor in my life. Several of the members encouraged me to consider ministry when it was not even a thought in my mind.

In addition to all that, the Pastor at the time, Dr. Buford Fordham, would leave the ministry to join the American Cancer Society. Fifteen years later he came back into the pastoral ministry to become my Associate Pastor of the First Baptist Church of Pasadena, California.

The Bible says: "God moves in mysterious ways, His wonders to perform." I have often said that verse should read: "God moves in **mischievous** ways, His wonders to perform."

Now, back to that first Sunday in Denver. That afternoon I returned to the Air Base and after lunch went back to the barracks. The young man who had the bunk next to mine was up by this time and asked me: "Where did you go this morning?"

"I went to church," I replied.

"Well, why didn't you invite me. I would have gone with you."

"Great. Go with me next Sunday. It is a wonderful fellowship." He agreed to go with me.

The following week was a busy one for me. The Korean War was ending and the need for B-29 gunners was lessening. Those of us in the Transit Barracks were scheduled to be given tests to discover our skills and aptitude for another career field. I can relate that at that time I did not know the difference between AC and DC current.

Nevertheless, the tests showed I had an aptitude for electronics.

I was placed in line to go to an Electronics School to learn to work on, and repair, the radar system on the Air Force's F-86D and F94C fighter aircraft.

The next Sunday morning, when it was time to get ready to go to church, the man in the next bunk, whose name was Nick Hunt, was still sleeping.

"Get up Nick, time to get ready to go to church."

"Hurrump . . . . mumble . . . mumble . . . go away," was the response.

"Come on, Nick, you said you wanted to go to church this morning. We just have time to get some breakfast before catching the bus."

"Go away, leave me alone, I'm sleeping."

With one quick flick of my wrist the covers came off his bunk. Nick jumped up with his hands balled into fists. He was ready to fight.

Stepping back I said, "Look, Nick, as long as you are up, let's go to church." Nick stood for a moment still half asleep and stunned to be standing in his skivvies in the aisle of the barracks. Finally he dropped his hands and said "OK."

So off we went to breakfast and then to the Main Gate. We took the same bus that transported this young southern boy the prior week. A constant vigil was kept looking for a stranger to appear again. No one did. It would never happen again.

Now, knowing when to pull the buzzer, we got off and walked up the two blocks to the church. What a difference a week can make. Not only was there no snow on the ground, there was green grass and birds were singing in the trees.

Now there were two members of the class who were in the military. Little did either of these two know that their future wives attended that church.

In that College-Career class was a young piano player whose name was Mary Ruth Elliot. She was to become Nick's wife and the mother to their three children.

As Nick and I returned to the barracks from church that afternoon, one of men who had a bunk down the aisle from us asked:

"What were you two fighting about this morning?"

We explained that we were not really fighting, only getting ready to go to church.

"Church", he said, "Why didn't you ask me? I would have gone with you."

In the following weeks it was discovered that many young men would go to church if they were invited. By the time July 4th came, there were two carloads of Airmen going to the City Park Baptist Church.

The "College-Career Class" had the name changed to the "College-Career-Service" class.

In June orders were given out for those in the Transit Barracks to go to their various schools. Electronics School was a difficult assignment for one with no background, or apparent interest, in electronics. The need was critical for the proper understanding of the important work to be done to keep our aircraft functioning.

In August my parents and younger brother drove from Alabama to Denver, Colorado for a visit. It was a grand time of reunion and celebration. They were pleased to see that the son who had left home weighing 220 pounds had slimmed down to 175. Even the uniforms had to be altered for a more slender figure.

My younger brother, Jim, seemed fascinated with Air Force life as we toured the Base, ate at some local restaurants and had a wonderful time of reunion. (Jim would eventually join the Air Force himself upon graduation from high school.)

That wonderful visit was short lived, however. Four days after my family's departure a message came to our Squadron headquarters that the Red Cross wanted me to call them.

The purpose of the call was to tell me of the death of my father. With no personal telephone number to call, my mother had to go through the Red Cross to reach me.

Mother told me of the return trip to Alabama. On the third day dad was not feeling well. Mother drove the last 200 miles. Upon arrival at their home mother went in to prepare dinner while dad lay down to rest.

When she went to call him to dinner, he had died.

An emergency leave was granted me to attend the funeral. Immediately after the funeral Mother and brother Jim moved to Miami to be near my sister Edith and her husband.

My Father had died at the age of 57 with lungs damaged from the war and with a bullet still in him.

Upon returning to Denver the feeling that comes from the loss of a parent was a present weight that lingered for several weeks.

As summer ended so did my loneliness. Beverly and I met at a youth meeting at the church. It was love at first sight for me and we dated as much as our schedules would allow. She was a student at the University of Denver where she was an excellent student, belonged to a sorority, and had many friends.

Beverly's father was a Federal Mediator-Conciliator who had been transfered to Denver after serving in Chicago, Sacramento, and El Paso. His job was to mediate conflicts between large corporations and labor unions.

Beverly's mother was a wonderful cook who said I reminded her of her favorite brother. Beverly's mother and I were very close.

On April 18, 1954 Beverly agreed to marriage. While her parents did not object to our marriage, they hoped for a long engagement. It seemed their wish would be granted since the next week graduation from Electronics School brought with it a promotion to Airman Second Class and a transfer to a new location, Tyndale Air Force Base in Panama City, Florida.

I left Denver and the love of my life for a new assignment in Florida.

A NEW ASSIGNMENT

THE HOUSING FOR single men was much better at Tyndale Air Force Base, which is just outside the city limits of Panama City, Florida. There were three assigned to a room. With more space for personal belongings, we spread out over the large room.

It was soon apparent that my witness as a Christian would fall on deaf ears. One of the roommates was already in a church, the other was not interested in any discussion of faith, politics and current events. His world revolved around movies and music.

His were hard habits to break.

Over my bunk was placed Beverly's picture, at which I looked as I would scratch out letter after letter to tell her how much she was missed and how much the future was anticipated. Her much longer, better written and more articulate letters brought a welcome relief from the lonely life of a stranger in a strange, new place.

Now with family 500 miles away in Miami, Florida, the possibility for frequent visits presented itself. There was, however, the matter of new duties which occupied much of my time. The shift assignment was from 4 p.m. until 11:30 p.m.. The task was to meet arriving F86-D fighter airplanes as they completed a training flight to ascertain the proper functioning of the radar. Some repairs could be made on the flight line, others necessitated removing a component for service in the repair shop.

THE SECOND VOICE OF GOD: THE CALL

THE FIRST SUNDAY at Tyndale AFB necessitated another bus trip. This time it was to downtown Panama City, about a 10 mile trip from the Air Base, where a large church spire signaled the location of the First Baptist Church of Panama City. The sign in front of this imposing structure listed Dr. Julius Avery, Pastor.

On this particular Sunday the Pastor, Dr. Avery, was not preaching. There was a visiting Evangelist whose sermon was on "the call to full-time Christian service." He listed several passages from the Bible about those who had been called of God.

There was Abraham, whose obedience led him to be called "father of the faithful." Then he gave a list of obedient men who heard and answered the call. Samuel and Jonah were the opposite in their response in the Old Testament. In the New Testament the preacher noted that Andrew and Peter, as well as Paul and Silas, were called of God and followed faithfully.

The sermon ended with an invitation to those who believed God was calling them to "full time Christian service" to come forward for a public declaration of their intent. The congregation sang "Just As I Am" all the way through.

The Evangelist said he was sure that there was someone in the congregation whom God was calling. We would sing the hymn again.

At that moment I knew he was talking to me.

I gripped the back of the pew in front of me to keep from going down the aisle.

As the congregation sang verse after verse of that old hymn, the visiting preacher would look directly at me, while I tried moving behind the person in front of me.

He would stop the singing to say again that someone was here whom God was calling. I held on to that pew with both hands. I was sweating. What was happening?

At last the service ended. Guess who was the first the leave the building?

Running across the street just in time to see a bus pull away from the bus stop, I would stand there for what turned out to be a 30 minute wait for another bus.

My mind was filled with questions about the feeling while holding onto the pew back. What is full-time Christian service? Is there such a thing as part-time Christian service? What was that pull going on inside? Was it the visiting preacher's persuasive voice or something else? How could he mean me? I am in the Air Force, engaged to be married, and living in a very regimented environment.

During the 30 minute wait for the next bus, Dr. Avery and the visiting preacher came out of the church building. The man with Dr. Avery looked at me across the street, got into the car, and while driving past the bus stop, turned and kept looking until the car was out of sight.

The next week was filled with adjusting to a new situation and duty station. I thought occasionally of the past Sunday service, but as the days went by there was less thought about the past and more about the future.

Word had arrived that Beverly and her parents were soon to be on their way to Florida. Her father had taken a medical retirement from Government Service and was contemplating moving to Ft. Lauderdale, Florida, 30 miles from Miami where my mother, sister, brother-in-law and brother lived.

The following Sunday came quickly. Getting ready to go to worship the roommates indicated their non-interest in attending. Knowing that Dr. Avery would be preaching, as he announced the prior Sunday, on the post-Resurrection appearances of Jesus, there was no pressure expected for a call to "full time Christian service" from such a sermon.

Surely the Evangelist had moved on.

The sermon was, as announced, that Jesus was called back to life by His Father. The grave is for the dead, not for the living. The invitation was given to any who felt dead to the Heavenly Father and who wanted the new life He gave.

Once again came the compulsion to go forward. Again the back of the pew was gripped. Hold on and hold out. If I could get through this hymn, I would be all right.

And at that moment God spoke to me for the second time in my life. Here are His Words to me:

"THE LONGER YOU HOLD BACK, THE LESS THE CALL WILL BE"

Now, this was not a warm feeling in my heart or a cold tingling in my toes. This was not a reflection of a thought or the culmination of a dream. This was reality.

Those were audible words, clearly articulated in my ear. I could now remember that it was the same voice I had heard at the age of 14.

How could this be? What did He mean? I was again confronted with wild emotions: God .... speaking to me? Was no one else able to hear that voice? I melted.

I was clinging again to the back of a pew.

I remember turning loose of the pew in front of me, but not how I got down the aisle.

The next thing I remember is standing before Dr. Avery. He asked me why I had come forward.

I told him I did not know.

"It's all right. God knows why you are here and we will pray for you."

And pray they did. The pastor and deacons gathered around to lift me up to our Heavenly Father. After what seemed a long time the "Amens" were said and the group parted.

I remember a mixture of feelings. The first was relief that I had been obedient even if it were late. Obedience is always blessed. But there was anxiety also. What did all this mean?

What about my engagement to Beverly? Would she understand that which I did not yet understand? Would she object to this decision? Was this an emotional reaction to circumstances I could not contemplate, much less articulate?

This I know. The critical factor in all this turmoil of thought and supposition was that of obedience. There are no boundaries or borders to being obedient; it needs no explanation to others.

Now I know that this was the "Secret Call" of God given to me in a specific way.

Looking back one can see that Samuel's call was in secret, heard only by himself.

Paul's call on the road to Damascus was personal and private, with his traveling companions unaware of what was happening even in their midst.

There was precedence in such a call. This was good company to be joining.

It was now the end of April and things were changing radically. Realizing there was a call is one thing, knowing what to do about it is another. Being new in the fellowship of First Baptist Church in Panama City meant that some time would be necessary to become better acquainted with the pastor and church leaders. I really was the new kid on the block.

In early May, Beverly and her parents arrived in Panama City on their way to Ft. Lauderdale. We had three days to spend in conversation and on the beach.

She heard about my decision to answer God's call. While she did not understand it either, she was not opposed to being married to someone who felt called of God. She said at one point that she had thought about missionary service herself.

Her parents were anxious to go on south to explore the region and to visit relatives. As we parted I was more sure than ever that Beverly was to be my wife, sooner rather than later.

Beverly's parents soon purchased a new house in Ft. Lauderdale, only 20 miles from where my mother and brother lived in North Miami. Plans were being made as to how we could spend more time together.

How would I be able to travel the almost 500 miles over the weekend? Because Panama City is north of Ft. Lauderdale and Miami, all the roads lead in that direction.

It was discovered that by putting on the summer khaki uniform and standing on the main highway that went by the Base, one could usually "thumb" a ride south. After the evening shift on Fridays, usually before 10 p.m., I would be dressed and ready to thumb my way south.

Beginning in June, and through August, I made the trip every other weekend. It usually took 10 hours in total rides, arriving in north Miami around 8 a.m. on a Saturday morning at my mother's house. Beverly and I would spend Saturday and Sunday together, sometimes with her parents and at other times with my mother. Usually only with each other.

Beverly started working as a salesperson at Burdines Department Store in Ft. Lauderdale. We both looked forward to Saturdays.

On Sunday evening the return trip was made. After being dropped off on Highway 27, Beverly would leave me until the next trip. The return trip took about the same amount of time which meant returning to Tyndale Air Force Base before 10 a.m. for a few hours sleep before the evening shift began.

These weekend trips meant that my time at First Baptist of Panama City was somewhat limited. Besides, a young man in love thinks of little else except the object of his affection. Our engagement lasted five months.

Our wedding took place at the First Baptist Church of Ft. Lauderdale, Florida on September 12, 1954. We had few earthly possessions – including all our wedding gifts – but our love for each other made the prospect of living in love for each other and with the grace of God surrounding us, a remarkable experience.

Our total income was $178.50 a month. Beverly insisted that we tithe that money. I was not sure we could live on $17.85 a month less. She said it was the right thing to do. She was right. Be obedient and be blessed.

Returning now to Panama City as husband and wife was both a thrill and a challenge. We joined the First Baptist Church of Panama City where we were soon asked to lead a group of high school young people. Being just a little older than our charges we sometimes acted like teenagers ourselves.

We rented an apartment from a member of another church while a new garage apartment was being completed nearby. This garage apartment had an upstairs as well as the ground floor apartment. We rented the ground floor apartment.

The apartment upstairs was rented by the newly appointed Associate Pastor of First Baptist Church, Billy Roberts who with his new bride, Jimmie Nell moved in just after we did. They were a delightful couple who exactly nine months after their wedding, welcomed their firstborn child.

We seldom saw each other except at church. My duties at the Air Base and our work with the youth filled our time.

My oldest brother, Roy, had presented us with an unexpected wedding gift of a much used 1940 Willis automobile. It took some time to get it running smoothly and long trips were very seldom attempted. It served to get me back and forth from our apartment to the Base for six months.

Dr. Avery and the Deacons had prayed about the future for this youth worker and voted to license me to preach in early 1955, citing the fact that God had bestowed upon this young acolyte the gifts necessary for the pastoral ministry. They were more sure about this than Beverly and I were, but we accepted the wisdom of the congregation even though the clarity they felt about us was not discerned by ourselves.

Life in Panama City was not always pleasant. We were newly-weds, apart from our birth families, living in a new place with no peer group. We were supposed to act like mature adults by guiding young people only 4 years younger than ourselves.

Our apartment, it was discovered later, had been built over a patch of ground which had been a "cricket farm" until recently. Crickets had been raised there for fishing bait. Even though a new building rested on the land, the crickets had not left. We discovered them in every room of the apartment and even upstairs to our neighbors, Billy and Jimmie Nell Robert's, apartment.

Both Beverly and I wanted a change. She wanted to get back to her college studies, and I desired advanced training in electronics.

It was mentioned earlier that on that first visit to City Park Baptist Church in Denver the man holding the door as I entered was Levi Floyd. It was Levi, who headed the Civilian Personnel at Lowry Air Force Base, who opened another door for us.

Mr. Floyd set into motion a series of recommendations that brought us back to Denver where I would enter an advanced electronics school. If was, in fact, one year from the day that I arrived in Panama City that orders came for my transfer back to Lowry Air Force Base.

We traded in the 1940 Willis for a 1947 Hudson Hornet which had enough room in the trunk and back seat to hold all our worldly possessions.

With the blessing of the church, we left Panama City on the long drive back to Denver. Beverly's parents had tired of Florida, sold their new home, and preceded us back to Denver.

God had provided a place for us to live while Beverly went back to college and I to more advanced electronic training.

Back in Denver we again attended City Park Baptist Church. The difference in this Baptist church and the one we had joined in Panama City was the denominational affiliation. The church which had licensed me to preach in Florida was a Southern Baptist church; the one in Denver was an American Baptist church.

There was some doctrinal differences which seem minor to those not connected with Baptist polity, but major to those inside the denominations. City Park, upon hearing that I had been licensed to preach by a Southern Baptist church, wanted to license me also. They wanted to encourage me to enter the ministry under the American Baptist egis. Thus, a second ceremony confirmed the license to preach in late 1955 by an American Baptist congregation.

While Beverly returned to her studies at the University of Denver, I was awaiting the start of my school when an officer of the school approached me about going to Instructor Training School.

It seemed that in my aptitude tests one of the strong components indicated the ability to convey accurate and competent information as a teacher. The decision was made for me to not only learn the advanced electronic data for the radar systems I had worked on at Tyndale Air Force Base, but to teach it to others.

To make this part of the story shorter, let it be known that not only did I become an Instructor in the school, but in a few months became a Shift Supervisor of other instructors.

In September, 1955 we became pregnant. It was good that we were back in Denver with a family doctor and with Beverly's parents who gave her prenatal care.

Our first daughter, Sheryl Gail, was born in May, 1956. She was a joy and a treasure, loved and adored by both her parents and her grandparents. Sheryl was the first grandchild to Joseph and Grace Vincent. They showered her with affection and attention.

Sheryl's grandparents were more than happy to take up the extra duties of caring for their grandchild while her parents were both in school. They were loving in both care and feeding.

When Sheryl was four months old Beverly and I drove on vacation to Los Angeles to visit with her relatives for a week. Sheryl did not seem to miss us while in the loving care of her grandparents.

In September, 1956 the opportunity presented itself for me to attend the University of Denver while still in the Air Force. The program was called "Operation Bootstrap", whereby military personnel could have their tuition paid if they attended a college where courses were offered to help advance them in their career field.

Since I was an instructor of electronics, taking a course in educational training was appropriate. I received a grade of A in the course. A second course in Introduction to Psychology resulted in the same grade.

In February, 1957 I completed my four years in the Air Force and started at the University of Denver as a full time student. Because of my grades I was given the Ballard Scholarship which covered part of the cost of tuition.

I began working at the *Denver Post* newspaper in the publicity department, which means I gave guided tours through the building to tourists. This part-time employment, along with the GI Bill and the Ballard Scholarship, meant that both Beverly and I had our tuition covered for us to complete our Bachelor of Arts degrees.

It was related earlier that Dr. Buford Fordham was the pastor at City Park Baptist Church in Denver, Colorado when I first visited there and he was the pastor upon our return. He called me into his office one day to tell me two things: First he said he believed that I was indeed being called to the pastoral ministry. The second thing he said that he was going to announce his resignation as pastor of the church to go with the American Cancer Society. This was an unexpected move on his part. He said his wife wanted a divorce, and the church would not want a divorced man to be pastor.

A Pulpit Committee was to be formed to call his successor. I was elected by the church to represent the younger members of the fellowship. After much prayer and interviews with several prospective pastors, we called the Rev. Alvin Johnson from Connecticut to be our new pastor.

Rev Johnson was a graduate of Yale Divinity School in New Haven, Connecticut.

During our course work at the University of Denver, Beverly and I took a course together in *Introduction to the New Testament* taught by the University Chaplain, Dr. William Rhodes who was, himself, a graduate of Yale Divinity School.

While these two men, Dr. Rhodes and Rev. Johnson, did not know each other, both were to influence our lives in different ways.

Upon accepting the call to pastor City Park Baptist Church, Rev. Johnson asked me to leave my work at the *Denver Post* and become the Minister to Youth at the church.

Beverly and I knew what such work entailed because of our earlier experience in Panama City. But, we did it anyway.

Other members of the congregation had been encouraging me to change my major in college away from preparation for Secondary Education and a career in teaching, and look to preparation for seminary. This would mean majoring in philosophy. I did not do this.

The vision Beverly and I had at that time was for both of us to be teachers in public education; she in the elementary school, I in high school. We were committed to education.

At the conclusion of one of our courses in college, the Chaplain, Dr. Rhodes asked me if I had heard of the Rockefeller Foundation Scholarship Program. I told him I knew nothing about such a program.

He said the Foundation was seeking out young men and women who had thought about going to seminary but were unsure about such a move. He indicated that, if approved, the recipient of the grant would be given a full year's tuition, room and board to an approved seminary. He encouraged me to apply.

Part of the requirements for application were to be approved by three fully accredited seminaries. I decided to apply to Berkley Baptist Seminary in Oakland, California, to Colgate-Rochester Divinity School in Rochester, New York and to Yale Divinity School in New Haven, Connecticut, (since both Rev. Johnson and Dr. Rhoades were graduates of Yale and, I had heard, so was the Chairperson of the local Rockefeller Committee, Rev. Harry Applewhite) Yale seemed an appropriate third choice.

I was excepted at all three schools. Then I met several times with the Rockefeller Committee. There were questions to answer, forms to fill out, and several interviews with various people.

But, to my great surprise, I was refused the grant on the grounds that "You have already decided to go to seminary whether we send you or not. This program is for the undecided." What a shock!

I was truly undecided then, but since I had been accepted for graduate work at all three seminaries, Beverly and I choose Yale for the purpose of graduate work with this rationale: Baptist seminaries would train pastors for Baptist pulpits, Yale, which is interdenominational, would offer the best all around training for whatever work God was calling us to do.

GRADUATION AND COMMENCEMENT

BEVERLY AND I graduated together from the University of Denver in August, 1959. We accepted the invitation to attend Yale Divinity School where we also acquired the last remaining apartment for married students on the Yale Divinity School campus.

Beverly was accepted as a first grade teacher at the new Deer Run Elementary School in East Haven, Conn.

Before graduating we sold our 1947 Hudson and bought a 1949 Buick. Now, with a newer automobile we were able to attach a U-Haul trailer for our clothes and household items. With our 3 year old daughter and a 10 year old car we headed for New Haven.

After our move to New Haven, Connecticut, Beverly's parents decided to move to California. They wanted a warmer climate. They had the warmth they liked in Florida, but did not like the humidity. They thought that Pasadena, California would be more to their liking.

Even without financial aid we were able to finance our seminary years. I did have one year left on my GI Bill benefits. Beverly's salary paid for Sheryl's day care costs, rent and groceries, and by securing a position with a local congregational church, my tuition was covered.

Sheryl was in a Day Center for the morning hours while Beverly taught her class. Most of my classes were in the morning also. I would pick Sheryl up, feed her lunch, put her down for a nap and do my studying.

Our first year at Yale was a challenge to all three of us. Beverly was a first-time teacher with 28 children whom she had to teach to read, write, express themselves in full sentences, and live together under her guidance.

Sheryl in a new environment, apart from her full-time grandparents, found that her Dad was not too good at brushing out her long hair, but did all right with macaroni and cheese. She endured it well.

For me the first year at seminary was a challenge. It was apparent that my focus on Psychology and American History while preparing for a secondary teaching position left me with large gaps for seminary preparation. Philosophy was a much needed course. I still had a lack of clarity of purpose and was deficient in creative thinking.

I had little appreciation for the setting in which God had placed us. We were overwhelmed with the whole Ivy League mentality and the rich history of Yale. My grades were mediocre and my focus on studies not sharp.

We survived our first year at YDS by determined effort and God's grace.

THE SUMMER VACATION WE NEEDED

IT WAS AT the conclusion of our first year at Yale, in 1960, that we sold our '49 Buick and bought a nearly new 1960 Volkswagen Beetle.

That summer we drove in our new car to California, stopping on the way to visit Beverly's relatives in Indiana and Illinois. Upon arriving in California Beverly's parents, the Vincents', smothered their daughter and granddaughter with pent up love and affection.

I had been asked to be the supply pastor at the First Baptist Church of Dania, Florida for the month of August. I left Beverly and Sheryl under the loving care of the Vincents, drove from California to Florida, and served for one month while the pastor, William Jennings, was on vacation.

Among the duties that awaited the supply pastor were preaching on Sunday mornings and Sunday evenings, leading the Bible Study on Wednesday night, teaching all the adult teachers the lesson for the coming Sunday, and teaching the Adult Mens Class. It was going to be a busy month. In my spare time I visited with my mother, sister, brother, and brother-in-law who also were members of that church.

Among the memories of that month of ministry one stands out:

On the first Sunday morning a middle-aged man was sitting on the very last row with his arms folded and a frown on his face. That evening the same man was sitting about half-way back in the sanctuary. On Wednesday evening he was on the second row for the Bible Study.

After the study was completed he came up to me and said:

"I am confused. They say that you are from Yale. Is that right?"

"Yes, that is right" I answered. "Why are you confused?"

"Well," he continued, "You seem all right. So, tell me, is it Yale or is it Harvard that is so bad?"

"It is Harvard", I said. "Well, that explains it. I am relieved."

So was I.

At the end of August I drove to New York to meet Beverly and Sheryl who took an airplane back from California. We then drove back to New Haven with our new appreciation of the people and place for work and study.

As we began our second year at Yale we ventured into New York City. We discovered that after a brief Saturday morning drive into the City we could park the car, attend the Radio City Music Hall for a movie, go to an AutoMat for lunch, see a Broadway Musical, eat at a good Italian restaurant and drive back to New Haven by 11 PM. We would repeat this Saturday routine several times over the next two years.

Our second year at Yale brought significant changes which were both challenging and charming. I had a new appreciation for the history of the place to which God had led us. We saw the opportunity to be joined in the task with His faithful servants for a fruitful ministry.

Beverly was being recognized as an outstanding teacher at Deer Run in East Haven. Sheryl entered her second year in Day Care without much anticipation, and I was a second year student who was being introduced to professors whose impact on my life is still being felt.

Among the professors were Dr. Roland Bainton in Church History. Dr. Brevard Child and Dr. B. Davie Napier in Old Testament. Dr. Paul Minear and Dr. Paul Schubert in New Testament. Dr. H. Richard Neibuhr in Ethics and Dr. William Muehl in Preaching.

Yale Divinity School has numbered countless scholars on its faculty. Those I have mentioned were giants to me. Another professor became my mentor.

The Rev. Mr. Samuel Reese Binch taught Baptist Polity at Yale Divinity School. He was Pastor of First Baptist Church in New Haven. He asked me to become his Assistant at the church to work with the youth. Under his guidance I began a true appreciation for pastoral ministry. He not only encouraged me to work with him as he prepared his sermons, he shared with me the struggles that come with faithful ministry.

In 1960 Sam allowed me to accompany him to the annual convention of American Baptist Churches in Philadelphia, Pennsylvania. We were there for the formal dedication of the new ABC headquarters in Valley Forge, Pennsylvania. We listened to Dr. Martin Luther King, Jr. tell of his vision for peaceful disobedience to unjust laws.

Among the things Dr. King said at that time was: "You can beat us, . . . and we will love you. You can turn the dogs on us, . . . and we will love you. You can kill us, . . . and we will love you. For the greatest power on earth is the love which comes from God."

We were now well established in the First Baptist Church of New Haven, and I enjoyed my apprenticeship under Rev. Binch.

THE THIRD VOICE OF GOD: CHALLENGE

THERE WERE THREE buildings on the Yale Divinity School campus for married students. Bellemy, Curtis and Fisher Halls were on the far edge of the campus. Each Hall had a janitor. I became janitor of Fisher Hall during our second year.

Fisher Hall, built on the side of a hill, was a sloping three level building with three entrances and five garbage rooms. My job was to shovel the snow from the entrances during the winter, sweep and mop the hallways, replace burned out lights, and empty the garbage three times a week.

It should be noted that these were the days before plastic garbage bags, garbage disposals in apartments and few vacuum cleaners.

The five garbage rooms each had two metal cans with lids for the residents to place their trash and garbage into. This included food scraps, coffee grounds, and all manner of refuse.

The apartments in the building were not air conditioned and the garbage rooms were not ventilated. There were often strong odors in the five garbage rooms, along with occasional ants and roaches.

Some of the students would sweep the dust from their rooms into the hallway. Through that year of emptying garbage, sweeping, mopping and replacing lights I was growing weary with the never ending task of picking up after sloppy people. It started getting hot in June. By July it was sweltering.

It was at this unlikely place and time that God spoke to me for the third time.

It was while standing in the middle of a hot, smelly garbage room with coffee grounds on the floor and two roaches on the wall and ants in the doorway that I blurted out – not so much in prayer as in frustration –

"Lord, I thought You had called me into ministry, and here I am with this stinking garbage."

And that is when the Lord spoke to me again, in clear words which came to my ears:

"If I cannot trust you with garbage how can I trust you with My people?"

You cannot imagine what those words did to me. It had been 13 years since His voice assured me of His love and of my significance.

It was the same voice in clear, articulate words. But, these words were not reassuring . . . . they were words with a question mark.

Here was the question I had to answer. Could I be trusted with small, everyday tasks?

Would God trust me in larger tasks? Will I be faithful, no matter the cause?

As I stood in that garbage room with my eyes on spilled garbage, ants and roaches, . . . my nostrils filled with the smell of decayed food, ... my ears ringing from a voice that astounded me . . . . and with sweat dripping down my body – . . . . I froze.

Here was God speaking to me again. Not in a car or in a church but in a garbage room. How could this be? What was I to do?

My delayed response was: "Yes, Lord."

I decided in that moment to become the best janitor that Fisher Hall ever had. The best custodian that Yale Divinity School ever had. The best worker I could possibly be.

I knew that an immediate change was necessary. The first order of business was the garbage rooms. I took all 10 cans out on the pavement, got a brush, a water hose and detergent and began scrubbing the cans. While they were drying I went to the five garbage rooms, swept and scrubbed them down. Next the cans were lined with newspapers and replaced in the rooms.

Over the next three days I swept and mopped the hallways then waxed the floors. I replaced all of the 60 watt bulbs with 100 watt bulbs. I sprayed the rooms with ant and roach killer and washed the windows on the entrance doors.

Within a week a remarkable transformation occurred in that building. Here are some about which there is first-hand knowledge:

With brighter, and shinier, hallways it became evident who was sweeping dust out into the hallway. This soon stopped as residents would sweep up the dust inside the apartment then put it into the waste basket.

With the garbage rooms cleaner the residents started wrapping their scraps of food and coffee grounds in neat newspaper packages and placing them into the cans,

With this change of behavior, my time spent in cleaning was cut in half, the building was cleaner and the residents happy.

The Supervisor of Building and Grounds for Yale Divinity School asked me to teach the other janitors how to keep a building clean and the residents happy.

Later that summer the crew from the Divinity School was put in charge of cleaning up many of the meeting halls and common rooms on the larger Yale Campus.

A CHANGE IN
MY THINKING

UPON REFLECTION ON all the influences that touched my life in seminary, that one brief moment in the garbage room is the seminal moment when I knew I was called into ministry.

I have been blessed and encouraged by professors, mentors, fellow students, church congregations and peers – but being called of God to be a better custodian with people's neglect and spilled garbage put new meaning into servanthood.

Course work took on new meaning. Theology and Church History came alive as I began to understand how the past impacts the present. Bible courses were anticipated now rather than endured.

I did not go to Yale to gain my faith in God. At Yale I found ways to understand what I believed.

As one theologian stated it: **"I believe in order that I may understand."**

As the only American Baptist in the senior class I had to defend what I understood to be "correct and proper" biblical principles. I defended adult baptism by immersion, communion being an ordinance rather than a sacrament, having a personal relationship with God through His Son, Jesus. I became a more informed and convinced Baptist by going to an interdenominational seminary.

In 1962 I received the Bachelor of Divinity Degree (BD) which was later changed to a Master of Divinity Degree (M.Div).

With renewed assurance of my call into pastoral ministry I was approved for a fourth year of study with an emphasis on "English Exegesis of the New Testament" which led to a second masters degree, Master of Sacred Theology (STM).

It was now our fourth year in New Haven. Beverly and I were concerned with the lack of physical exercise for Sheryl in the cold climate of Connecticut. Beverly enrolled Sheryl in a children's dance class at the local YMCA. After a few weeks the teacher said: "Sheryl is a natural dancer. When you get to your new location you must get her into a proper dance school. She has the talent and ability to become an accomplished dancer".

Well, of course, we would think about it. More about that, later.

During graduation ceremonies in 1963 I carried the Divinity School flag as all the different schools of Yale (Law, Medicine, Music, Architecture etc.) met on the Commons for the Commencement address before the degrees were conferred.

The Commencement speaker that year was President John F. Kennedy. It is the custom to confer an honorary doctorate degree on a distinguished speaker. This was done to Kennedy whereupon he said:

"Now I have the best of both worlds. A Harvard education and a Yale degree."

As we were leaving the Commons and each school going back to our separate campuses, one of my friends who had received his doctorate was talking with other people and not watching where he was going. He stepped off the curb and into the street where a taxi driver slammed on his brakes to avoid hitting him and shouted out of his window "Watch out where you are going you nut." At which my friend, holding up his degree certificate, said "Doctor Nut."

In May, 1963 the annual convention of American Baptist Churches was held in Detroit, Michigan. I was the only American Baptist student at Yale that year. There were two distinguished graduates of YDS, Dr. Howard Moody and Dr. Dean Wright, who were placed in strategic positions in the denomination. One called to say that the Ministers and Missionaries Board of the ABC would pay my convention expenses to Detroit in order to meet the Executive Ministers of the States to which I might be interested in placement. While in Detroit I met Dr. Charles R. Bell, Jr., Pastor of the First Baptist Church of Pasadena, California. It was in this church that my in-laws, the Vincents, had their membership.

Dr. Bell was cordial but guarded in his reply to my inquiry about staff needs.

I talked with the Executive Minister of So. California, Dr. George Downing, who indicated that the likely hood of a recent graduate of Yale coming to California was slim. His advice was to find placement in Ohio, then Kansas, and then in a few years applying to come on West. His logic was that few Baptist churches in the West would want to go to the expense of bringing out an unknown graduate from an interdenominational seminary.

I returned to New Haven to finish the last of my course work. I declined the opportunity to candidate for positions to pastor churches in Connecticut, in New Jersey and New York. We were determined to seek placement in California in spite of the odds.

Upon returning from the Detroit convention, I met with the Board of Deacons of the First Baptist Church of New Haven who recommended to the Ordination Council of the American Baptist Churches of Connecticut that I be ordained. After a thorough examination by the council, approval was given for ordination to the gospel ministry of Jesus Christ.

Rev. Samuel R. Binch, Pastor of First Baptist Church of New Haven, Connecticut, led the service where the "laying on of hands" by all the ordained persons there blessed my calling to the pastorate.

WE GO WEST TO CALIFORNIA

IN THE SECOND week of July, 1963 we stored all of our belongings on the stage of the First Baptist Church of New Haven and packed our suitcases in our Volkswagen Bug to head for California without a clue as to where God was calling us.

Sheryl, now 7 years old looked forward to having the back seat to herself for the trip. Such was not to be, however.

As we were preparing to leave New Haven Sam Binch, our pastor, knowing that we were traveling West asked for a ride to the Canadian Border, Windsor, near Detroit. His brother, who was a pilot for Canadian Airlines, would meet him for a ride back to their mother's home in Canada.

There were four of us who traveled to Detroit. There we left Sam Binch, having arrived at Niagara Falls at midnight just after the flood lights were turned off. I lifted Sheryl up and said: "Listen to the Falls, honey."

Leaving Detroit we traveled south to Evansville, Indiana where Beverly's aunt and uncle lived with her two cousins. The older cousin had just completed high school. As a present to her we offered to take her with us to visit her other relatives in California. Sheryl was willing to share the back seat with Julie. Now there were four of us again.

We next stopped in Herrin, Illinois, Beverly's birthplace, to visit an elderly aunt who had been widowed for over 10 years. As we sat in her house telling about our trip, Aunt Maude said:

"Well, I guess I will never get to California."

Whereupon Beverly said:

"Why don't you go with us?"

"All right" replied Aunt Maude, "I believe I will."

While Maude packed her suitcase I went to a local hardware store and bought a luggage rack and a cover for the Volkswagen. All of our suitcases were rearranged. The items we would not need for the trip went on top. Everything else was stored under the front trunk or behind the rear seat.

Now there were five of us in the VW with Sheryl, Julie and Maude in the back seat.

It was an exciting trip West. We stopped in St. Louis and Denver for visits with relatives and friends.

This was July, the weather got hotter as we traveled West and by the time we got to New Mexico, crossing the desert with no air conditioning in the car, with the hot wind blowing through the car, Beverly suddenly had a craving for "chili"! Then we knew the feeling of her uneasiness was not because of the heat or the crowded automobile.

Beverly was pregnant.

We arrived safely in California. Maude and Julie went to stay with other relatives while the Vincents welcomed us into their home. After a good time of visiting around, Maude and Julie returned to their homes. Both were to later say that trip was the most wonderful time of their lives.

My time in California for the month of August was spent in interviews. It seems there was an open position for an Assistant Pastor of the First Baptist Church of Pasadena.

Dr. Charles R. Bell, Jr. formed a search committee. After several meetings I was called to that position which I began the first of September, 1963.

We rented an apartment close to Beverly's parents while we looked for a house to buy. My duties at the church included being in charge of evangelistic outreach, visiting the sick and shut-ins,teaching an adult class, counseling, and occasionally, preaching.

I served as AssociatePastor at the First Baptist Church of Pasadnea from 1963 until 1968.

In November of that first year,while in a counseling session, the church secretary informed me that John F. Kennedy had been shot. It had only been six months prior to that date that we heard him speak at Yale. It was unbelievable to think the President was dead.

Our second daughter, Shauna Grace, was born in February, 1964. She was a wonderful delight from the moment of her birth. That summer we bought our first house in Pasadena. It was there that Shauna learned to walk, then run. She hasn't stopped running to this day.

The Minister's Council of Southern California elected me to be Secretary, then Vice President, then President for the State. Later I was elected to be Vice President of the National Minister's Council. This meant annual trips to Green Lake, Wisconsin to our Assembly Grounds and to Valley Forge, our National Headquarters. The Minister's Council was instrumental in making many changes in denominational life during these years.

TWO DANCING
DAUGHTERS

AS WE MOVED into our new house our daughter, Sheryl, enrolled in the Girl's Club for an after school dance class. It was there that Sheryl's teacher confirmed what the teacher in New Haven said, "Sheryl is a dancer. Get her enrolled in a proper dance school."

Beverly placed Sheryl with a French ballet teacher in a nearby community. There Sheryl continued to grow in her ability while Shauna, our younger daughter now three years old, wanted to dance also. Beverly took both girls to the studio for ballet lessons each week.

The next step for both girls was to enter the Pasadena Dance Theater under the leadership of Evelyn LeMone. In a brief time Sheryl was accepted into the Senior division of the Pasadena Dance Theatre while Shauna became a member of the Junior Company.

They both continued there until Sheryl started going into Los Angeles, 15 miles from Pasadena, to take lessons from teachers who had been in Broadway Shows and taught classes intended to shape professional dancers. Sheryl won scholarships to continue her lessons.

While in high school, Sheryl was in several musical presentations where she sang as well as danced. Upon completion of high school Sheryl entered Citrus College where she was part of a singing group, the Citrus Singers.

Sheryl still continued her trips into Los Angeles for dance instruction, representing her studio at auditions for professional shows and touring companies as part of her scholarship responsibilities.

In 1968 Charles R. Bell retired as Pastor of the church. I was one of several candidates who were interviewed for the position of Pastor. I was called in April, 1968 to that position. I would be the youngest Pastor in the history of that church. I desired an older man to be my Associate Pastor.

As I prayed about this decision, the name Buford Fordham kept coming to mind. You may remember his name from the year 1953 when he was Pastor of City Park Baptist Church in Denver, Colorado. This was the same pastor who called me into his office to tell me that he believed that I was being called into ministry. This was followed by his announcement that he was leaving ministry because his wife wanted a divorce. He joined the American Cancer Society after leaving the church. I had not heard of him, or from him, in fifteen years.

After several letters and telephone calls he acknowledged that he had been in prayer about his relationship with the Lord and his place in His service. Dr. Fordham had attended an E. Stanley Jones Conference and rededicated his life to God. He had met the widow of a Methodist minister, fell in love, and was recently married.

Dr. Fordham agreed to preach my Installation Service. While in Pasadena he met with our Pastoral Search Committee and agreed to accept the call to become the Associate Pastor of First Baptist, Pasadena.

THE FOURTH VOICE OF GOD: COMMAND

It was in that same year, 1968, that I was in New York following a meeting of the Ministers Council. It had been five years since leaving Yale and our frequent Saturday visits to New York. I was interested to see again the places we knew. Everything seemed changed.

The streets were not clean and the Theater District was run down. Times Square was the most deteriorated. There were porno shops and prostitutes, drug dealers and panhandlers everywhere one looked.

I was shaking my head as I was leaving the district when I noticed an African American man standing on an upside down Coca Cola create. He was holding an open Bible and preaching. He was saying:

"Don't go down that street", (the one I had just left).

"Down that street is Satan's Hell hole, the Devil's playground.

It is dark, dismal, dank and dirty. It is full of deceit and disease.

Don't go down that street."

I was in agreement with him. In my head and heart I knew he was right. I had seen what he was talking about.

It was that moment that God spoke to me again. Let me repeat that. God spoke to me again. I heard His voice in my ear. The sound was louder than the street traffic, louder than the shuffle of feet of people passing by, louder than all the sounds of New York City. I heard His voice say to me:

"GO, STAND BY THAT MAN"

"What", I said out loud. Looking around me for the source of that voice. I saw no one who was looking at me, or even close enough for me to have heard them speak.

Again, He spoke the same five words:

"GO, STAND BY THAT MAN"

I stood there, frozen. I had been given a command. I was told to do something.

I knew what I was supposed to do. I was supposed to go stand by that street preacher on that New York corner. My head was spinning about what to do!

Can you believe that! . . . . But I did . . . . I thought to myself: Here you are, Bill, the newly called pastor of a prestigeous church in Pasadena, California. You are a graduate of Yale Divinity School. You are well dressed and too theologically astute to place yourself by some ranting street preacher in New York.

With my head down, I started walking away.

Words cannot describe my feeling of failure. I had been called by God to affirm someone else. To authenticate his message by my presence, by standing with him and affirming the truth about what he was saying.

Talk about defeat, despair, discouragement, disappointment. I knew them all.

How often I have wished that I could go back to that time and place and make amends for my disobedience. But no one can go back. Failure is a part of life. Would God ever trust me again? Was failure to be part of my future?

As I walked away from that corner I ran my tongue over the chipped tooth I received on the ball field at the beginning of second grade when I disobeyed my teacher's instruction. Would there be another scar to mark this act of disobedience?

Now, back to Pasadena to take up the role of Senior Pastor to a large church. No one can live under the shadow of defeat when Christ is in one's life. I would just have to leave my failure in New York and continue the ministry to which I had been called.

By the late 1960's and early 70's there was a growing drug culture in Southern California. Eaton Canyon, in Sierra Madre, California, had become a haven for hippies and drop-outs. I joined with two other pastors, and several laypersons, to minister to the young and old who had "turned on and dropped out."

We held Bible studies in the Canyon and a Saturday night service in an Episcopal church in Sierra Madre. We saw God's hand in many miracles, as there were professions of faith followed by changed lives.

Another ministry was begun for ex-convicts. One of the lay people from the Canyon ministry introduced me to Nick and Pauline Cadena. This couple was part of Victory Outreach. They started a half-way house in Pasadena for ex-convicts. We partnered with them to reach those who were trying to adjust to life outside the walls of prison.

This ministry to ex-convicts led to another ministry. This time to those who were still in prison. It was called – "Match to Man." This ministry meant visits to local jails and prisons where a match between one on the inside and one on the outside corresponded with each other.

This ministry was not confined to men only. Since women were also included in the ministry it became known simply as: "M2."

My wife, Beverly, was part of this ministry also. One day while visiting the Women's Division in Chino State Prison in East Los Angeles, she discovered that she had locked her keys in the car.

Reporting this news to the Gate Guard she was told that there was no problem. Calling to one of the trustees who was working in the flower garden the guard asked the convict to "help the lady get into her car."

With no apparent tool or effort the door was quickly open with the words to my wife: "There you go, lady."

Over the years Pasadena has become known as the home of the Huntington Museum, Cal-Tech, Jet Propulsion Laboratory, the Rose Bowl and Tournament of Roses Parade.

Since the First Baptist Church was one block off the parade route, our congregation would host other church groups by placing chairs along the parade route as well as providing coffee and hot chocolate and doughnuts for the police force on New Years Eve.

By 1970 "The Jesus People" ministry was gaining strength. Our congregation became active in this outreach.

Duane Petersen head of the "Jesus People" movement was an effective voice to the young people who were caught in protest to almost everything that the "establishment" held dear.

The ministry grew to the point where the American Bible Society published a special edition of the New Testament *Good News For Modern Man* with the phrase "Key 73" on the cover. That cover had a picture of the Rose Parade on it.

On New Years' Eve 1972 over 1800 young people crowded the sanctuary of the First Baptist Church of Pasadena for a mid-night communion service, then took copies of the "Key 73" New Testament to distribute to those who were standing and sitting on the Rose Parade route on Colorado Boulevard. What a night!

BIG CHANGES WERE ABOUT TO HAPPEN

BY 1975 OUR daughter Sheryl had graduated from high school and entered Citrus College where she was immediately chosen to join the "Citrus Singers" a well known and talented group selected from the music department of the college.

Sheryl had continued her dance lessons in Los Angeles and would represent her studio when auditions were announced for local venues or touring groups. She was one of hundreds who auditioned for the Alice Cooper 1975 tour of his new album **"Welcome to My Nightmare."** She was one of four dancers chosen for her ballet ability to accompany the tour company.

Perhaps you can imagine the prayerful and deliberate thought Beverly and I gave to allow our 19 year old daughter to drop out of college to go on a several months tour with a Rock group, especially one with the man named Alice Cooper. His family named him Vincent Damon Furnier at birth. He changed his name legally to "Alice Cooper" when the band was formed.

We gave our permission, but how could we know that Sheryl and Alice Cooper would fall in love?

Following the tour, and now back in Los Angeles, Alice courted Sheryl even when we were on a family vacation. He asked me for Sheryl's hand in marriage.

My response was "I cannot give my daughter's hand in marriage to a man who had not given his life to Christ."

"My father is a pastor" he said, "and I was raised in the church. I know what it means to surrender my life to Christ. I would have to give up too much at this point." He acknowledged my reluctance to give my blessing by promising to read the Bible every day and to pray with Sheryl every day.

With that assurance, we gave our permission and blessed the union. Alice's father, Mick Furnier, and I officiated at their wedding ceremony in March, 1976.

Alice, true to his word, did read the Bible and pray with Sheryl. They later moved to Phoenix, Arizona where, after attending a large church in Phoenix, Arizona they selected a smaller church in Scottsdale. It was there that Alice made his profession of faith in Christ and was baptized.

As of this writing they have been married 32 years and have three children: Calico, Dash and Sonora. They live in Arizona.

The year 1976 was a turning point in all our lives. Sheryl married Alice Cooper.

It was the year of the Bicentennial with celebrations all over the nation.

It was the year Jimmy Carter was elected President.

It was the year of memorable change in Pasadena for our family.

It was mid-morning on a Saturday in early September. I was standing on a ladder pruning a tree in our front yard. Something hit me in the back of the head. My hand flew up to see if I was bleeding while I looked around to discover whether someone had thrown a rock at me.

No one was there. I checked for a swelling, thinking I had been stung by a bee. Nothing there. Suddenly I became nauseous. I went into the house to lie down. A tremendous headache was building with no relief and after two hours of resting with three aspirins, I knew I was in trouble.

Beverly called the Associate Pastor, Buford Fordham, to prepare him for the possibility that he might be preaching for me on Sunday. Friends recommended a doctor, but he was not available until Monday. Sunday I could not move or even get out of bed.

With no let up in the headache I was driven to the doctor's office early Monday morning. A series of tests in his office revealed nothing.

I was admitted to the hospital where a whole series of tests were run. In the late afternoon the doctor informed me that there was only one test left to perform; a spinal tap. When the spinal tap was done, my headache started to subside.

The results of that test revealed that I had contracted a viral infection of the spine, a form of spinal meningitis. The doctor said that the area of the brain where spinal fluid is manufactured had an infection.

There was nothing that could be done about it. The doctor indicated there would be one of three consequences:

I would die

I would be partially paralyzed

I would live with no bad effects.

I was released from the hospital two days later. The doctor called several times over the next three weeks to see if there were any ill effects. I was healed by God's grace.

Nothing gets one to probe deeply into the meaning and purpose of life like a life threatening illness. It took several days to regain any strength. My mind seemed to be clear but my planning process was sluggish.

THE FIFTH VOICE OF GOD: COMMITMENT

ONE MONTH AFTER my hospital stay I awakened one morning in panic. I did not know what to do. When I say do, I mean exactly that. I had no vision for the church.

My preaching schedule for the coming weeks leading up to Christmas had been worked out, but now I was unclear about what to preach. I tried to go over in my mind what needed to be done in the areas of mission, ministry, building, visitation, teacher training, evangelism .... nothing came into focus.

That is when I prayed specifically for God's help in decision making. What was I to do?

It was in that early morning hour that God's voice came again to my ear. Clearly, audibly, without announcement or warning. Here is what He said to me:

"You will never be able to be faithful to Me until you say 'No' to Pasadena."

I lay in the bed without moving. The room was vibrant with energy. My ears were alive with the echoing sound of His voice. It was October and suddenly it felt like summer. I was sweating, my breathing was labored and my heart was beating rapidly.

That same voice I had heard in Alabama, Florida, Connecticut and New York had found me in California. God not only knows my name but my inner thoughts. I had not remembered this feeling of His closeness since my act of disobedience on a street corner in New York City in 1968.

Now, what did He mean?

The idea that I was holding on to Pasadena like a life preserver had never occurred to me. It was true that over the past ten years I had several inquiries about accepting a call to another church. I had invitations to consider other pastorates in California as well as churches in the mid-west and eastern areas of the country.

Each time I would consider where I was now and compare the new possibility to Pasadena. I would decline each invitation. What could be better than where I was serving now? Sheryl was married, Shauna was excelling in dance and musical theatre, Beverly had her parents living nearby, the ministry was growing and the congregation was pleased. Why even consider another place?

When God spoke to me that morning I knew what He meant. I was content with contentment. I was concerned with 'doing' instead of 'being'. He had called me to be faithful and I was concerned with success.

Some have said it was my illness which caused my disquietude, that I was just tired or feeling burned out. Whatever the cause I now had to answer the question implicit in God's statement that early morning hour.

I had to say NO to Pasadena.

I called a special meeting of the Board of Deacons. I told them that I was resigning as Pastor. They wanted to know why I was leaving. Was there something they could do to change my mind? Did I need a raise in salary? More vacation? More staff?

My response to their heartfelt concern: "There is nothing for you to do."

My question to them, "Do you want a 30 day, a 60 day, or a 90 day notice?" It was now the last Saturday in October. They asked for at least a 90 day notice. It was agreed that I would conclude my ministry at Pasadena First Baptist Church on January 30, 1977.

A BIG DECISION WAS MADE – NOW THE CONSEQUENCES

NOW, WHAT TO do? I was back to "doing" again. But, how could I "be" faithful without "doing" something? I prayed . . . . a lot. I was asking God for guidance, wisdom, discernment, understanding.

What had I done to my wife and daughter? Where would we get money on which to live? I had 90 days to the end of a pay check. I was not worried, but I was concerned.

Call it a lack of faith, but how was I to know what God wanted from me? At least I let it be known through denominational headquarters that I had resigned the pastorate and was ready for the next step in ministry.

In the month of November three different churches contacted me. Each one was in a different state and would mean a different life style from the one we had been living for the past 13 years.

I had mentioned previously that over the past few years I had been contacted by several churches about a possible move. One of the more interesting conversations with the chairman of one Pulpit Committee went something like this:

"Pastor Goddard, we would like for you to consider becoming our pastor."

I replied, "Thank you, but I am happy in Pasadena and not wanting to make a move."

"Oh, we know that. We would not want someone who wanted to move.

We think we can make you an offer that would change your mind."

I wondered if they were still looking for a pastor. Perhaps I was too hasty and cavalier in my response to that offer a year ago.

Shallow thinking. But, at least I was thinking.

In early December I accepted an invitation to meet the Pulpit Committee at a large church in the East. This church was east of Illinois where I had interviewed earlier. (I will not name any names in order to protect the guilty.)

It was an impressive structure, with a large congregation in an affluent neighborhood of a major city. I had questions about the staff, the By-Laws of governance, and the mission statement of the church. After a two hour session I knew that this was not where God wanted me to minister. It was a liberal church with, (in my estimation), little regard for the full gospel of Jesus Christ.

As I told them I knew I was not the pastor for this church, I asked why they had asked me back for this interview. The chairman was very blunt and to the point:

"You know that last month Jimmy Carter was elected President."

"Yes", I replied.

"Jimmy Carter is a Southern Baptist. There are many prominent Southern Baptists in this neighborhood. We want a pastor who can bring that group into the church. Therefore, we want a pastor with an Ivy League education and a Southern Baptist background. You fit the bill."

They had done their homework. We seemed a likely fit on paper. So much for computerized placement without prayerful consideration of the person.

Another church who had contacted me about the possibility of an interview in November, called to let me know they had selected the man they were calling to be their pastor. They would not need to interview me.

I was visiting my mother in the hospital when the Vice Chairman of that same church called to ask me to come to Oak Park, Illinois, a suburb of Chicago, Illinois for an interview. It seems that the person they had asked to become pastor had said no. "He had a better offer." The committee was somewhat miffed over that statement.

I accepted the opportunity to go back for an interview, thinking all the while that one of the churches I had interviewed in Chicago, and then withdrawn my name from consideration, meant that I was saying 'no' to Chicago. I had to change my mind.

My first question to the Oak Park committee was "Why me?" I knew the person to whom they had offered the first call. We were so different I could not understand their reasoning.

One of the members, in answer to my question, said: "God alone knows."

She was right. Only God knows why anyone of us is chosen for His flock.

On February 6, 1977 I became Pastor of the Oak Park, Illinois First Baptist Church. How could I know that while I was preaching that Sunday morning, my mother would die.

Her suffering was over as my new ministry was beginning. It was a Communion Sunday. We ended the service by singing "Blest be the Tie That Binds."

Absent in the body, at home with the Lord.

It had been six days after completing the ministry in Pasadena that I started the ministry in Oak Park.

Beverly and Shauna stayed in Pasadena, California. Beverly to sell our house and Shauna to finish the school year. Part of my contract with the church was the understanding that I could enter McCormick Theological Seminary on the campus of the University of Chicago, to work on my Doctor of Ministry Degree. I began my first course in March.

Shauna was 13 years old and not happy with her father for transporting her from the only home she had known, from friends she did not want to leave, from the Pasadena Dance Theater, to an older community just outside of Chicago where she would be a stranger without friends and no known Dance Studio at which to study.

Beverly began immediately to redecorate the parsonage. Shauna made a few friends, but still missed her old ones.

Beverly scouted out the Dance Studios in the area and would take Shauna across town to Evanston to one studio and then into Chicago to the Ruth Page Studio.

It did not take long for a Chicagoian to ask Shauna to join his new company "The Hubbard Street Dancers". Shauna was one of four girls, and at 14 the youngest professional dancer in the country.

The next years The Oak Park/River Forest High School, where Shauna was enrolled, made special provisions for Shauna to take morning classes, then journey to downtown Chicago for her dancing; giving her credit for "physical education"

THE SIXTH VOICE OF GOD: COVERING

IN SEPTEMBER, 1977 the new school year began. Vacation time was over and the activities of the church were underway. The last Sunday in the month was another turning point in my life.

It was at the conclusion of the morning worship hour. Standing on the steps outside the front door of the church, I was greeting the parishioners as they left. As I was about to turn and go back inside I was grabbed by a young, heavy set, dark haired man who had bounded up the steps and said:

"Hello, Pastor, my name is Andy Gonzalez and Jesus sent me here." As I looked at this broadly grinning Latino, God spoke to me, saying:

"Cover That Man"

I froze, again. That same Voice. The Voice I first heard at age 14.

The same Voice at the First Baptist Church in Panama City.

The same Voice I heard in the garbage room at Yale Divinity School.

The Voice that commanded me on the street in New York City.

The same Voice I had heard before resigning from Pasadena First Baptist Church.

This was the sixth time I heard God speak to me. Audibly, clearly, intentionally, personally. I heard Him say to me "Cover that man."

Simply that and nothing more. Nothing more was needed to be said. I knew what He meant. I knew what I was to do.

"Yes, Lord" was my response

God was giving me a second chance to obey Him. It was 10 years prior to this meeting with Andy Gonzalez that God had spoken to me on a street corner in Times Square of New York City when listening to an African American, street preacher, He told me to "Go, Stand By That Man." I was disobedient. I had walked on by.

Now, without a moment's hesitation, I embraced this man and said:

"Welcome, brother Andy, you are at home." I meant that. If Jesus had sent Andy to us in Oak Park, then I was to cover him in any way that God directed.

Andy was to be my redemption from the failure to obey God 10 years ago. I would be obedient now.

Cover him I did.

I learned in the next few weeks that Andy had grown up in East Los Angeles in a Barrio where drugs, guns, prostitution, gang activity and poverty were part of daily life.

Andy participated to such an extent in that life that he spent a majority of his young life behind bars. I learned that he knew Nick and Pauline Cadena with whom I had ministered in Pasadena.

He knew of Victory Outreach and, it turned out, was in the Chino State Prison next to the Women's Division the day Beverly locked her keys in the car.

Andy Gonzalez was one of God's special agents. A convicted criminal who had his life changed while behind prison bars. Thank God for those who go to minister to the sick, the lonely, the prisoner.

Andy had been witnessed to about the penalty of sin and the forgiveness of sin that Jesus Christ can bring to one's life. Andy surrendered to the call of Christ while behind bars.

When released from prison, Andy went to a Victory Outreach and then to a ranch in Arkansas where he was told that he was being called to minister to those behind bars who, like himself, had never surrendered to Jesus. After a brief time in Arkansas, Andy came to Chicago.

Andy enrolled in Emmaus Bible School, a Plymouth Brethren school, which was housed just across the street from First Baptist, Oak Park. When asked why he came across the street to a Baptist church, Andy would only say: "Jesus sent me here."

Jesus sent him and I was to cover him. That is a simple statement that covers a multitude of obligations and opportunities. The only similarity I could find between us was that we were both redeemed by a loving God who looked beyond our past failures and loved us in spite of ourselves.

When I think of Andy and me I am reminded of an older church father who, while praying, said to the Lord:

**"How Thou canst think so well of me, and be the God Thou art,
Is darkness to my intellect, but sunshine to my heart."**

It seemed the only thing that Andy and I held in common was the uncommon love in which God held us. We were brothers in Christ . . . We had the same Father.

Without a formal education, Andy had a native intelligence, an inquiring mind, a loving heart, a steadfast desire to be faithful to his call, and was completely free from the fear of failure. He would venture where others were afraid to go.

His explanation of this freedom from fear was that Jesus had conquered all our enemies. "What have I to fear", he would say, "I am a Jesus man."

Andy invited me to preach at a morning Chapel service at Emmaus Bible School early in 1978. It seems the administrators were somewhat skeptical of a Baptist preacher leading the worship at their school. Andy assured them that "Reverend Goddard is my Pastor. He is OK." I preached. We prayed. God was glorified. We survived.

My introduction to the prison ministry was more traumatic. Andy invited me to go with him to the Cook County Jail.

He had been cleared a few weeks prior and wanted me to preach to the prisoners one Friday night. After being cleared at the gate, we proceeded to the dinning room where every table and stool was bolted to the floor.

This was not my first experience behind bars, but it was my first experience in preaching to the inmates. As the men began to stream into the room there was much talking, laughing and chatter.

Andy yelled out: "Be quiet and be seated."

One inmate called out: "I've got something I want to say."

To which Andy replied: "You shut up and sit down. We are here to teach you. You are not here to teach us."

Turning to me, Andy whispered: "You've got to be tough with them Pastor." Then, when they were seated, Andy told them that he had brought a man who knew everything there was to know about faith in Jesus.

Here he is, Pastor Goddard.

Then, whispering again to me, Andy said, "Sic um pastor."

I have no idea what text was used or exactly what was said that night.

This was a congregation with whom I could not identify. How could I sing the Lord's song in a strange land?

This was Andy's congregation. They spoke the same language and shared experiences different from my own. All I can remember of that message was that "God loves you. Jesus died for you. You can be forgiven if you confess your sins and find freedom on the inside of your spirit even while your body remains inside these walls."

That night we prayed with five men to find forgiveness through confession of sin and to accept the grace of God through Christ. Andy's comment to me as we were leaving the Cook County Jail that night was, "You did good, pastor."

My covering Andy did not mean that I shared his passion for preaching in prison. As I prayed about what God asked me to do in relation to Andy my feeling, – and I repeat, feeling, since I had no direct verbal instructions – , was to encourage, challenge and defend him before schools, congregations and seminaries.

We put Andy in the First Baptist Church's Mission Budget and commissioned him as our Home Missionary. When our Board of Deacons was ready to ordain Andy, the Chicago Baptist Association informed our church that Andy did not have the credentials to be recognized as an American Baptist Minister.

Our response was, "He is God's man. He has a recognized ministry. We will ordain him whether or not you recognize him as such." This we did. Andy proved steadfast in his determination to be trained and recognized as a minister of Jesus Christ to those being held captive by Satan behind prison bars.

He received a certificate of attendance from Emmaus, attended classes at Northern Baptist Theological Seminary and earned his degree from McCormick Theological Seminary in Chicago.

The Chicago Baptist Association did recognize Andy's ministry and even put "The Cook County Jail Ministry" in to the Region's budget. Several churches in the the CBA, as well as churches from other denominations joined the ministry.

From one of those churches Andy met a young, shy, deeply spiritual young lady whose name was Marjean. They shared a desire to be faithful in the prison ministry.

They both were committed to the Lord's work. Individually they were very effective. As a team they were terrific. Love followed friendship and shared ministry. Andy and Marjean were joined in marriage at the First Baptist Church of Oak Park, in a wonderfully spiritual service at which I had the privilege to officiate.

Much more could be written about the prison ministry at Cook County Jail, although the founder of that ministry, Andy Gonzalez, is no longer with us.

Andy died in 1996. His widow, Marjean Gonzalez was ordained by the Oak Park First Baptist Church to continue that ministry. She is a faithful follower of Jesus and obedient to His call.

One way to know that any movement or ministry is valued and valuable is that it outlives its founder. This is true of this ministry which celebrated 30 years of faithfulness in November, 2008.

WORKING TOWARD
MY DOCTOR'S DEGREE

THE THREE YEARS from 1978 through 1980 were full of new activities at First Baptist Church Oak Park. These activities concerned the work the congregation did in partnership with me as we worked toward the D.Min degree at McCormick Theological Seminary in Chicago.

The congregation had agreed that the new pastor could work on an advanced degree. What I had not known at the time of the call to the pastorate was that this church was a merger of three Baptist congregations.

I was the first pastor the merged church had called. The pastor who facilitated the merger, Dr. Ray Johnson, had died of a heart attack just before his retirement. His motivation in the merger was to save the First Baptist Church of Oak Park by inviting the First Baptist Church of Austin, which had been merged with the Second Baptist Church of Chicago, to join with the fellowship at Oak Park.

It soon became apparent that the merger was in body but not in soul or spirit. There were still three separate groups of people who had not been fully vested in the new fellowship. Strangers in a strange, new land.

A brief history to set the scene:

Second Baptist of Chicago was established July 4, 1864. It was during the Civil War and the first pastor, Dr. Edgar Goodspeed, was opposed to slavery. The church was the only downtown church building to survive the Chicago Fire of 1871.

That fire left thousands homeless. The church building was used for a week to house many of the homeless while many members took others into their houses. Over 17,000 homes were destroyed, 300 died, with many missing. Over 100,000 were left without houses and 73 miles of city street frontage was destroyed.

During a ten year period, Second Baptist formed eight new churches in the area.

First Baptist of Austin was formed in 1871 by members of Second Baptist and others who were moving west for a new beginning following the "Great Fire."

First Baptist Oak Park was founded on May 9, 1873, again with several members of Second Baptist who had moved into the western suburbs.

By 1874 Second Baptist was the largest white Baptist congregation in the world until Charles H. Spurgeon's time in London, England.

In 1913 the Northern Baptist Theological Seminary was founded in the basement of Second Baptist Church while John Marvin Dean was pastor. It was John Marvin Dean who became Northern Seminary's first President.

In January, 1972 the merger of Austin-Second and Oak Park First Baptist was completed. The first two congregations brought 274 members to add to Oak Park's 390.

So many differences among the three fellowships had not been addressed. With each church feeling the loss of members and declining finances, the mode of worship, the place of young people, and leadership style became areas of disagreement.

It was now five years since the merger. Very little progress had been made in being a community of faithful followers. It was as if there had been a "burial" of the two former churches without a eulogy or funeral. Their past history was forgotten and the future was uncertain. The merger had been one of necessity. Now what?

It was into this scene that God called me to minister. What a challenge. What an opportunity. McCormick Theological Seminary was offering a degree program which emphasized the revitalization of existing churches. It was into that program that I enrolled in March, 1977.

The question I brought to my course work was: "How can I, as pastor, bring the influence necessary to bond three groups into one fellowship?" Through the three-year course work I found several answers.

Reuel Howe in his book, *The Miracle of Dialogue*, says the answer is simple:

"They become a community when as persons, the members enter into dialogue with one another and assume responsibility for their common life." (page 5)

It was through the Doctoral Program that I attended classes, wrote papers, interviewed parishioners, read books, and began looking seriously at what the possibilities were for forming a new fellowship out of three separate congregations.

Under the guidance of my supervising professor, Dr. Edward F. Campbell, Jr., I chose an Old Testament model to manage this merger. It was Dr. Martin Noth in his book, *The History of Israel*, who called attention to the episode of Joshua at Shechem who called the 12 tribes together and led them through a commitment service, called for a new covenant, and established a series of celebrations to mark the nation of Israel.

This would be the model chosen for the Austin-Second-Oak Park merger. The title of my Doctoral Thesis was:

"From Shechem to the Suburbs: Managing A Merger."

Using the biblical model of Israel becoming a community under covenant with its celebrations, this project dealt with the importance of forming a corporate memory in merger, adopting a covenant to define the faith of the community, and to stress the importance of celebration in congregational life.

This was an 18 month process during which a new covenant was formed, new hymnals bought, new choir robes were purchased, the by-laws of the church were changed and new committees replaced old ones. The celebrations honored the past ministry and mission of each of the three churches.

We adopted each others' history and memories. We joined together forming a fellowship out of a "gathering of strangers". Bible study became exciting and worship took on a glorious time of praise and proclamation.

McCormick Theological Seminary conferred the Doctor of Ministry degree (D.Min) in March, 1980.

In the next years new opportunities for ministry opened. I was asked to serve on the Board of Trustees of Northern Baptist Theological Seminary. While serving on the Board I was asked to become Adjunct Professor of Preaching. In addition, I became Chairman of the Board.

Other duties included serving on the Board of the Baptist Retirement Home in nearby Maywood, Illinois as well as on committees of the Chicago Baptist Association, with special attention to the Cook County Jail Ministry.

In 1984 the church honored my seventh year of pastorate by allowing a sabbatical leave in the summer to study in Oxford, England. While there I completed the work of writing the devotional pages for a large-print hymnal by Hope Publishing Company.

The devotional pages were placed among hymns by various authors with themes for the church year. The title of this hymnal: "Wonderful Words of Life" is still being sold and used in many nursing homes and retirement centers.

While all of this was going on, Shauna, a member of the Hubbard Street Dance Company, was becoming well known as the company started touring.

When a senior in high school, Shauna was chosen as "Presidential Scholar", one of two from Illinois and one of 100 from the whole nation. We accompanied her to Washington D.C. for her award at the State Department where a reception was held in honor of all the recipients, complete with a citation signed by President Ronald Reagan.

Shauna was awarded two scholarships: The Carniege Scholarship and one from the National Foundation for the Performing Arts Scholarship. To cap the week, she danced at the Kennedy Center for Performing Arts.

Shauna was asked to perform in several National Academy of the Arts venues. She was continuing her touring with the Hubbard Street Dancers. When Hubbard Street played at the campus of the University of California in Los Angeles, Shauna decided that UCLA was the place she wanted to go to earn her college degree.

She was accepted and graduated in 1989 with her major in Communications and a Bachelors of Art degree.

Shauna performed in two movies and made several television commercials before going to Europe. She lived and worked in Rome and Milan, Italy before starting her own studio in Monte Carlo, Monaco.

A CHANGE IN MINISTRY

THAT SAME YEAR was a transition in Oak Park for Beverly and me. The Baptist Retirement Home, on whose Board I served, was severely hurt by the organization of a Union among the workers at the Home. Picket lines ringed the property.

Milk and meat could not be delivered, nor could the garbage be picked up, because of the pickets. The Administrator was forced to resign.

Residents were having tires slashed and the police, also Union members, did little to help. No new applications were coming in while the stress of the months long strike caused some residents to move, others died.

I cannot say it was the Lord's leading as much as my own ego which led me to accept the call to become the Administrator of the Home during this crisis. I really believed I could make a difference.

On June 3, 1989 I resigned as Pastor of FBC Oak Park to take up a new and very different ministry.

Some things did improve over the next 18 months. The strike was settled with the workers in the kitchen and maintenance departments getting an extra twenty-five cents an hour pay increase and their birthday off from work. What a very little was realized for the few, while so much hardship came to the many.

While more personal and pastoral attention was given to the present residents, very few new applications were made. It was decided to give the administration of the Home over to the American Baptist Homes of the Midwest. A professional management team came on board.

I resigned after 18 months and looked to God for guidance for the future.

In March, 1991, I accepted the call to become the Interim Pastor of a newly founded Baptist church in Sacramento, California.

This was a small and struggling congregation which responded to the gospel of Jesus with open arms. After much prayer and deliberation, Beverly and I accepted their call to be full time Pastor of the Southside Comunity Church of Sacramento, California. This we did in November, 1991.

For the next nine years we loved and were loved in return. The congregation grew, a second worship hour was added. Land was acquired for expansion, new staff members were employed, the music ministry blossomed. God is good, all the time.

THE SEVENTH VOICE OF GOD: CONTEMPLATION

I HAVE BEEN RELUCTANT to come to the telling of this seventh, and as far as I know, the last time God spoke to me. This time there was no evident meaning to the voice. Oh, I heard the voice just as in the past six times. It was clear, articulate, personal and understandable. Well, let me tell what happened.

It was at 11: 00 am on a morning in middle March, 1999. I was driving in my car on the way back to the church after making a hospital call. I was thinking about the parishioner I had just prayed with in the hospital.

There was very little traffic on the road that day. As I was driving and silently praying, God spoke these words:

"TURN LEFT AT THE NEXT CORNER"

It was as if someone were sitting next to me in the passenger seat. The voice was in my right ear. It was clearly spoken, articulate and unforgettable.

The same voice of my childhood, my youth, my adult years. It had been 20 years since I had heard that voice, but it was the same voice

I took my foot off the accelerator. Gripping the steering wheel, I looked in the rear view mirror. Nothing there.

Without thinking of anything else other than obedience, I flipped on the left directional signal and coasted until I came to the next corner. It was a residential street with no traffic signal or stop sign.

I turned left on the street and pulled to the curb and stopped. My heart was beating faster. I was breathing with some difficulty. I waited.

No other direction was given. I looked around me at the houses on the corner, then down the street. No visible signs of life. Now, what was I supposed to do? I waited for awhile to let my heart rate slow down, all the while looking for something visible to catch my attention. Nothing.

I began driving slowly down that street. Looking left. Looking right. Expecting someone to be walking down the side walk or standing by the curb or sitting on a porch.

There was no one else on that block.

I continued driving. Another block. Nothing. I looked in the rear view mirror. Nothing. My heart was still racing. What did this mean I was to do? I kept driving slowly until the street ended at a major intersection.

I stopped at the corner waiting for more direction. Silence. Perhaps if I waited at that intersection someone would pull up behind me. No one did. Cars were going by on the street in front of me. I could not just sit there. Which direction to turn?

To the left would take me back to the church. To the right toward our house. My thinking was to go home. It was nearly noon and Beverly would have lunch ready. I drove to the house and went inside. Immediately Beverly said,

"What is wrong? You are as white as a sheet."

I told her about the voice and the instruction I was given. She was as puzzled as I. We talked about the possible meaning for me to turn left at the next corner. The voice did not say 'at the next intersection, or the next traffic light, or the next stop sign', but at the next corner. Which I did.

There is only conjecture now. Was I to turn left, not to see someone, but to avoid an accident? Was I being prevented from going on into something from which I was being protected?

To this day I do not understand why I was told to turn. I only know that I did as I was told. I was obedient without knowing why.

LOOKING BACK IN REFLECTION

Over the years, as I have taught Bible study in several congregations, I have said that there are always three questions to be asked about any passage in the Bible:

What does it say?

What does it mean?

What does it mean to me?

The first question has to do with construction of the Word. We attempt to come as close as possible to the exact wording in the original language. Translations can make a difference in what we read or see. Hebrew, Greek, Aramaic, English have different words for the same concept. In what language was the Word first given? What does the Word say?

This is known as **Exegesis.**

The second question has to do with the understanding of those to whom the

Word was first addressed. How did they interpret the meaning of that Word in their life, in their context, in their time? What was their response?

This is known as **Exposition.**

The third question has to do with **Application.** How am I to not only understand what was originally said and understood by the first recipients, but how am I to make this Word relevant in my life, in my context, in my time?

When the written Word of God becomes personal to me, relevant in my context, then that is God's Word addressed to me. A response is always demanded.

LOOKING FOR THE MEANING

AS I HAVE gone through the pain and pleasure of reflection over the seven times God spoke to me, I have some thoughts I would like to pass on to you as you read this.

I have given, as clearly as I know how, my answer to the first two questions about what did God "say" and what did He "mean".

Now, to the third question, the application.

REFLECTION ON THE FIRST TIME GOD SPOKE TO ME

"IT DOES NOT MATTER HOW YOU GOT HERE,
IT IS TO WHOM YOU BELONG NOW."

That was the first time I heard God speak to Me.

I was a confused and conflicted 14 year old boy when I first heard God speak to me. I questioned my identity and purpose. I was miserable about my weight gain and the lack of understanding and acceptance by my father.

To me this Word from God was a Word of Comfort

God said I was somebody. I counted. I made a difference to Him. He loved me.

The joy that swept over me is almost indescribable in words. I can try to describe for you my feelings, but no words could express the full meaning of God's voice to me that night.

There was a feeling of euphoria that enveloped me. I had literally heard God's voice, and I felt that "something" was lifting me up from that automobile seat. It felt as if I were able to float, no matter how much weight I had gained.

For the first time in my life I felt that I belonged. That my life counted. That I was loved without having to deserve it or earn it. Long before Thomas Harris wrote the book: *I'M O.K, YOU'ER O.K,* I knew that was true. For me. In that car.

That night my existence was settled for good and forever. I knew then what it meant to be accepted by God. I was His son, by adoption, through baptism. That feeling, that knowledge has always remained with me. I have never doubted God's love or my worthiness.

What does this mean to you?

Through my years in ministry I have met many men and women who do not know who they are. They are lost.

My way of describing lostness is when you do not own your past, you cannot define your present, and you are unable to plan your future, ... you are lost.

You are lost to the love and service of God in Christ Who came to redeem your past, bless your present, and give you an eternal hope for the future.

I have counseled both men and women who do not know their birth parents.

They were raised in an orphanage or adopted by someone who gave them a name. Some believe that they were "accidents" or "unplanned" for by parents who tolerated them but did not love them.

Some were told that they were "illegitimate". One has related that she was told that she was the product of rape and "lucky to be alive".

My response to them is always to repeat what God said to me:

"It does not matter how you got here, it is to Whom you belong now".

That means you, also. No matter the circumstances of your birth you were given God's most precious gift, human life. What you do with what God gives you makes an eternal difference.

Think back to Samuel who was "abandoned" by his mother to live with an elderly man in a distant place from home. When God called, he answered:

"Speak Lord, for Your servant is listening"

REFLECTION ON THE SECOND TIME GOD SPOKE TO ME

The second time God spoke to me was not in an automobile but in church. Remember, I was holding on to the back of the pew in front of me as He spoke:

"THE LONGER YOU HOLD BACK THE LESS THE CALL WILL BE."

That Word from the Lord I understood as my Call.

H. Richard Neiburh in his book: ***THE PURPOSE OF THE CHURCH AND ITS MINISTRY,*** describes the four aspects to the call for ministry. He notes that the **first call is the call to be a Christian.** Everyone has received that call.

Have you had God call to you? Yes, you have. Through His written word, through His Living Word (Jesus) God calls you to be His special child. You were born once – no matter the circumstances, the time or the place – you were born.

Now, you must be born again. Yes, again. The first time was a physical birth. You are your parents child no matter who they are. To become God's child you need a spiritual birth.

When you were conceived you were given a spirit along with your body. Your spirit was given to you to have communication with God. If you don't have communication with God, your spirit withers. God sent His Son into the world to bring Life, full and abundant. A new spirit.

As someone said: **"Born once, die twice. Born twice, die once".**

The question you have to answer is: "To Whom do I belong"?

There is an old expression among Christians that we have "surrendered" to God. What else could that mean but to "give up" trying to live a meaningful life apart from God. When you surrender you put your hands up.

One of the old church fathers said:

"He is no fool to give up that which he cannot keep, to gain that which he cannot lose".

My prayer is that you become a brother or sister in Christ to me. That depends upon whether or not we have the same Father. If you know Jesus as your Lord and Savior then we are related.

Welcome to the Family of God.

Neibuhr goes on to describe the **second call** in ministry as **"The Secret Call"**.

That is the intimate, personal call to an individual for a specialized place of service in the Kingdom. It is difficult if not impossible to describe to someone who has not experienced that aspect of the call.

That happened to me on a Sunday morning in a church in Panama City, Florida. It was real. It was in secret. It was personal.

Now what does this mean for you?

Some of you have probably received that call also. But you held on so long to something tangible that the call was less and less, until it was gone.

Maybe it wasn't the back of a pew but some relationship or job.

Many have related to me how one thing or another kept them from faithful service when they knew God called them. To one it was an engagement for marriage, another a job offer in his father's firm, another said it was a desire for a promotion in a new business, another confessed the fear of being called to be a missionary in a foreign land.

How many have been lost to useful service in God's kingdom because something more enticing, exciting or rewarding was offered. Fear is a factor also. The fear of failure, fear of the future, or fear of the Lord has deterred many.

The **third** aspect of the call, according to Neibuhr, is **"The Providential Call"**.

He means that God equips those who are called to His service. You have the gifts for the certain ministry to which He calls you. You will not be sent to where you are not equipped to go. Not everyone is equipped to be an evangelist, or a foreign missionary, or a preacher. But, everyone is called to be a witness to the love of God in Christ.

The **fourth** aspect of the call which Neibuhr notes is **"The Eccleslastical Call".**

The call of the Church. And, to Neibuhr, this is the final test of the call to ministry. If the Church does not authenticate your call, you are not called, says Neibuhr. It is the stamp of the Body of Christ which recognizes the validity of the call.

For some this means Ordination, for others a Commission. For all it means a devotion to service in the name of God for His people.

REFLECTION ON THE THIRD VOICE OF GOD

The third time God spoke to me was while I was preparing for ministry in seminary, working as a janitor in a smelly garbage room. God answered my complaint about being misplaced as a minister in training while working with garbage by saying to me:

"If I cannot trust you with garbage how can I trust you with My people."

I understood this Word to be one of Challenge.

What that meant to me was that God expects my best effort no matter the job. I was on trial with a menial and unrewarding everyday task. How does one prepare for more responsibility but by being responsible in small things.

Does this have any meaning for you? Have you failed to see that the common, everyday tasks are to be done to glorify God? Think about that . . . . Every job, small or large, gives us the opportunity to demonstrate our faithfulness. God is watching every move and decision you and I make. He cares about the small things. We should too.

Here is a thought . . .

The purpose of every Christian is to "live to the praise of His glory."

Your job . . . right now . . . where you are placed . . . offers you an opportunity for God's blessing. Don't miss the blessing by thinking that your job is insignificant or that it does not make a difference.

God is watching us, trying to catch us doing the right thing. You do not want to disappoint God by doing sloppy work.

REFLECTION ON THE FOURTH TIME GOD SPOKE TO ME

You will remember that I was in New York City, leaving Times Square, seeing a street preacher admonishing passers by to avoid the path of darkness and destruction.

God spoke to me these words:

"GO, STAND BY THAT MAN"

This was not a word to comfort, or to call, or to a commitment. This was a command.

I have already related what those words meant to me. Do they have any application in your life?

Do you ever make a judgment about the worthiness of another person? Do you ever consider yourself more important or more significant than someone else? Do you have prejudice about race or gender? If so, then you are a member of a large fraternity.

I was treating this street preacher they way I had treated garbage before God spoke to me about my attitude. I did not want to touch or handle or even stand close to him. I had changed my attitude about garbage but not about people.

How stupid could I be? I had not made the connection about how to treat any person – black, white, male, female, rich, poor, educated, illiterate, well dressed or in rags – as a person of worth because each is created in God's image and loved through Jesus.

I hope and pray that you are not as stupid as I was at that time. If you are, then now is the time to change your attitude.

I considered myself to be better than a black street preacher. Wrong. He, too, is a child of God. He needed someone to stand by him, to affirm his truthful words, his warning to the multitude. I was chosen, by command, and I failed the Commander.

Are you being challenged to stand by someone other than yourself? I admonish you to consider that you are a significant person whose influence will make a difference in another's life. Don't miss the opportunity to stand up for Jesus anywhere His name is being lifted up. If you are not obedient, you will miss a blessing.

REFLECTION ON THE FIFTH TIME GOD SPOKE TO ME

It was an early morning in September, 1976 that God said to me:

"You will never be faithful to Me until you say 'NO' to Pasadena."

This Word was a word to test my Commitment.

I related my stunned feeling and lack of immediate comprehension to that voice. I then realized that my affection for the setting in Pasadena was blocking any other possibility for faithful ministry. I settled for success rather than faithfulness.

I reported my decision to resign to the Board of Deacons. I had become vulnerable. I had made a decision to be obedient no matter the cost. But was that fair to my family? Beverly made the statement that no trapeze artist turns loose of one swing without knowing that there would be another swing to catch as you are falling.

I was in free fall.

What does this mean to you? I cannot say what it means to you, if anything. But ask yourself: "What am I holding onto for meaning and purpose in life?". If you have staked your reliance on place or position or income or anything else that you can taste, touch or feel, then how can you know you are open to God's call?

In the book of Genesis Abraham was told to leave his father's home and journey to a distant land about which he knew nothing. By his obedience, Abraham became known as "father of the faithful."

Faith is established through obedience. That is where the blessing lies.

REFLECTION ON THE SIXTH TIME GOD SPOKE TO ME

It was less than a year later that God spoke to me again. This was the shortest interval of all between voices. I had relocated from Pasadena, California to Oak Park, Illinois. It was a Sunday morning following the worship service while standing on the outside church steps when a young Latino introduced himself to me.

God said to me: "COVER THAT MAN".

A clear voice in my ear. An immediate recognition to His meaning. God was giving me a second chance to be obedient by affirming another person. No matter how different we were, here was a brother in Christ whom Jesus sent to my doorstep. This time my response would be different.

The black street preacher was my first opportunity. Andy was my second opportunity. I did not want to let this second chance pass me by.

What does this mean to you? Remember that personal applications can only be done by the person who understands the message. There is an old expression which has new meaning. One person tells another "I've got your back". That means one can go on without worrying about anything or anyone blindsiding him because someone has his back covered. Have you been asked to cover someone?

Perhaps your recommendation could help someone advance. Perhaps there is one who needs your encouragement or advice. Perhaps there is someone who can do a better job with your help.

Here's a thought: **"There is no limit to the amount of good which can be done, if you don't mind who gets the credit."**

Someone may be waiting for you to give an encouraging word, or a kick in the pants.

REFLECTION ON THE SEVENTH TIME GOD SPOKE TO ME:

A WORD FOR CONTEMPLATION

The last time I heard God's voice still leaves me with questions.

I have related what was "said" and "what that meant". I was obedient. I was told to; "Turn at the next corner." That I did. But why? What was I to do then?

One of the most difficult things for Christians to do is to be faithful in all situations. We seek reasons for our decisions, meaning and purpose to our deeds. Who wants to be blindly obedient without knowing "why"?

In the Old Testament story of Jonah we read that Jonah was told by God to go in one particular direction to a certain destination. Jonah went in the opposite direction. He acted contrary to the voice of God. There is a lesson there. Jonah was a reluctant prophet who became fish food. God had to transport him against his will in order to do what he had been instructed to do.

In the New Testament we read that Jesus and His disciples were invited to a wedding feast. When the wine was all gone Mary, Jesus' mother, came to Him and asked Him to do something. Jesus replied "My time is not yet come", to which Mary turned to the servants and said to them:

"Whatsoever He says for you to do . . . . do it".

Mary's word to the servants at a wedding feast on that long ago day is the word we all need to hear in this day: "Whatsoever He says for you to do . . . . do it".

I did, not knowing why.

However God's Word comes to you . . . in written form or spoken verbally, you are to be obedient without knowing why in order to receive a blessing. What blessing? That is a mystery to me to this very day. But, this I know, God knows best what I need to do. Do you know that for yourself? My prayer is that all of us will be obedient to His voice.

EPILOGUE

THESE ARE THE seven times I have heard God speak to me. Perhaps He will again before I die. If not, then at that time my hope and prayer is to hear Him say to me what He said to a man in one of His parables:

> "Well done, good and faithful servant. You have been faithful in small things. I will make you faithful over large things. Come, enter the joy of your Master." (Matthew 25: 21)

POSTSCRIPT

A FEW WORDS ARE in order about my family.

Beverly and I have been married 54 years. We are retired and living in Florida.

Sheryl, our oldest daughter, married Rock Star Alice Cooper. His name was officially changed from Vincent Furnier when he started his band. They have three children, Calico, Dash and Sonora, and live in Arizona.

Shauna, our youngest daughter, graduated from UCLA and started her career in Europe. She lived in Rome and Milan in Italy. She later opened two businesses in Monte Carlo, Monaco. Shauna now lives with her husband, John Barger and her two children, Christopher and Sophia, in California.

A few words are in order about your response to what I have written.

For thousands of years people have said they "hear voices". Some have said these voices tell them to do strange or horrendous things. There are people, in both mental institutions and in society at large, who believe God, or someone else, is speaking to them. About them I do not know.

Perhaps you have heard God speak to you. I have talked with three people since I began writing this account who have told me that God spoke to them in a particular instance.

I believe that when God speaks He does not tell us to act in ways which are contrary to His written Word or to His character revealed in Jesus Christ.

If you have had an experience of God speaking to you and have never had anyone with whom to share that great moment, I would appreciate hearing from you.

My e-mail address is . . . . novemberbill@juno.com

May the love of God the Father, the grace of the Lord Jesus, and the fellowship of His Holy Spirit lift you up and lead you on in the faith which comes to those who are obedient to His Word. Amen

REFERENCES

Brevard S. Childs Memory and Tradition in Israel. London: SCM Press, 1961

William H. Goddard Wonderful Words of Life. Hope Publishing Co. 1985

Reuel L. Howe The Miracle of Dialogue. The Seabury Press. 1963

H. Richard Niebuhr The Purpose of the Church and its Ministry. Harper and Brothers, 1956

Dr. Martin Noth. The History of Israel. New York: Harper & Row, 1960.

Dr. William H. Goddard. From Shechem To The Suburbs. McCormick Theological Library. 1980.